Millennials are People Too!!!

We must give US millennials the help they need to live the American Dream

No generation as a whole in history has ever been subject to the ridicule that is meted out to millennials on a daily basis.

Some say millennials deserve the put-downs and some say they don't. In the midst of all these put-downs of the "snowflake" generation, it sure seems one big fact has been lost: Millennials are people too! And, they are a lot nicer than most other people think.

That does not mean that they do not deserve the rap that they have gotten. Think about the story of the Yale Professor who had to give his suffering students an optional midterm because they were upset with Donald Trump's victory. Online comments about this were plentiful with the usual mocks about the snowflake generation, the spoiled, entitled babies, raised to love only themselves, coddled by their parents and adorned with participation trophies that everybody received.

Growing up in the age of social media made this generation obsessed with instant gratification. Things have gone bad for millennials as they reached adult-hood and even before. They need again the kind of great reinforcement that they had in T-Ball through adolescence when the participation trophies were the rage. Today, they get their kicks by being rewarded with online actions such as a "like" or "retweet." The US workplace was not ready for millennials and maybe that's why, so many are still unemployed. Of course, it might also be that foreign nationals took their jobs.

At work, if they can find a job, needy millennials like that feely-good stuff just like the social "likes" and "retweets." They'll even settle for constructive criticism if that's all a peer can muster but they would prefer lots of reinforcement or praise, especially from a manager. This need was not in their original genes; but the need seeped in as dose after dose, feely-good stuff was always the remedy. Even good dads had a hard time denying them.

Millennials are known as the selfish generation. It is said that they need to look up the meaning of the word, friend, each time somebody accuses them of being one. They are tarred with being the lazy and entitled generation, because from my observations, they often behave that way. Sometimes I wonder if I am the only one who sees it?

Maybe they have a really valid beef with life. Their generation is saddled with $1.45 billion in student loan debt. That would keep many smiles down. This book is written for the flawless millennials, so they can see their flaws as others see them and know why they have them. It is written for moms and dads and kindergarten teachers and lots of others, hoping that we never put out a group of participation trophy winners like this ever again. This author believes that being a millennial is not a terminal disease and the more the patient knows about herself, the easier the cure will be.

BRIAN W. KELLY

Disclaimer: Though judicious care was taken throughout the writing and the publication of this work that the information contained herein is accurate, there is no expressed or implied warranty that all information in this book is 100% correct. Therefore, neither LETS GO PUBLISH, nor the author accepts liability for any use of this work.

Trademarks: A number of products and names referenced in this book are trade names and trademarks of their respective companies.

Referenced Material: *The information in this book has been obtained through personal and third-party observations, interviews, and copious research. Where unique information has been provided or extracted from other sources, those sources are acknowledged within the text of the book itself or at the end of the chapter in the Sources Section. Thus, there are no formal footnotes nor is there a bibliography section. Any picture that does not have a source was taken from various sites on the Internet with no credit attached. If resource owners would like credit in the next printing, please email publisher.*

Published by: LETS GO PUBLISH!
Publisher: Brian P. Kelly
Editor: Brian P. Kelly
P.O Box 621 Wilkes-Barre, PA   www.letsgopublish.com
Library of Congress Copyright Information Pending
Book Cover Design by Brian W. Kelly; Editing by Brian P. Kelly

ISBN Information: The International Standard Book Number (ISBN) is a unique machine-readable identification number, which marks any book unmistakably. The ISBN is the clear standard in the book industry. 159 countries and territories are officially ISBN members. The Official ISBN For this book is also on the outside cover: **978-1-947402-47-8**

The price for this work is: **$9.95 USD**

10   9   8   7   6   5   4   3   2   1

Release Date: August 2018

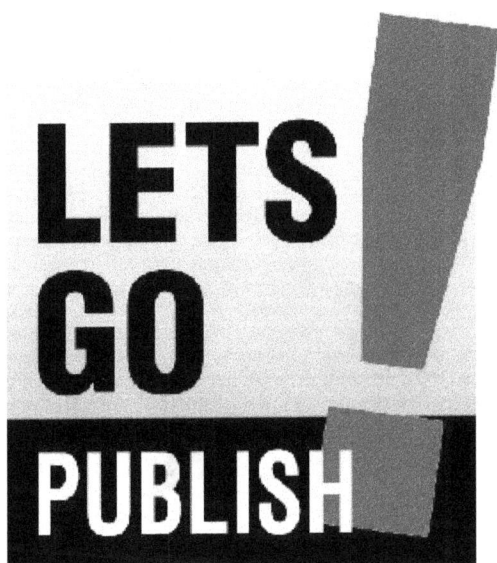

Dedication

I dedicate this book to my wonderful wife Patricia; our three wonderful children Brian, Mike and Katie; and our friendly friends—Ben our very happy dog, who recently became an Angel, and Buddy, our always cheerful cat.

Thank You All!

Acknowledgments

I appreciate all the help that I have received in putting this book together as well as all of my other 135 other published books.

My printed acknowledgments had become so large that book readers "complained" about going through too many pages to get to page one of the text.

And, so to permit me more flexibility, I put my acknowledgment list online, and it continues to grow. Believe it or not, it once cost about a dollar more to print each book.

Thank you and God bless you all for your help.

Please check out www.letsgopublish.com to read the latest version of my heartfelt acknowledgments updated for this book. FYI, Wily Ky Eyely loves this book and recommends it to all. Click the bottom of the Main menu!

Thank you all!

Preface:

Rarely does a book title explain exactly what a book is about. This book is an exception. Once we know that millennials really are people, then we know that they deserve to be treated like all other people. Since that has not worked well for millennials over the years, we use a subtitle to discuss the solution "We must give US millennials the help they need to live the American Dream." I'll be the first to say that understanding what happened to them will be easier than getting these young Americans out of the corners they built for themselves over their short lives.

No generation as a whole in history has ever been subject to the ridicule that is meted out to millennials on a daily basis. Many Some say millennials deserve the put-downs and many say they do not. In the midst of all these put-downs of the "snowflake" generation, it sure seems one big fact has been lost: Millennials are people too! And, they are a lot nicer people than most other people think.

That does not mean that they do not deserve the rap that they have gotten. I still remember the supposed myth of the Yale Professor who had to give his suffering students an optional midterm because they were upset with Donald Trump's election victory. Online comments about this were plentiful with the usual mocks about the snowflake generation, the spoiled, entitled babies, raised to love only themselves, coddled by their parents, with rooms adorned with all of the participation trophies they received for unusual acts such as breathing.

Growing up in the age of social media made this generation obsessed with instant gratification. Things have gone bad for millennials as they reached adult-hood and even before. They definitely need help as the rumors of their behavior have caused many Americans to dread the day they would go face to face with a millennial.

It is up to the Baby Boomer generation to make them whole again as they are not living real lives today. They need the same reinforcement therapy they got in T-Ball when the participation trophies were the rage. Today, they get their kicks by being rewarded with online actions such as a "like" or "retweet."

They and not well employed compared to other generations as the US workplace was not ready for millennials and so many are still unemployed. Of course, it might also be that foreign nationals, working for less took their jobs.

At work, if they can find a job, needy millennials like that feely-good stuff just like the social "likes" and "retweets." They'll even settle for constructive criticism if that's all a peer can muster but they would prefer lots of reinforcement or praise, especially from a manager. This need was not in their original genes; but the need seeped in as dose after dose, feely-good stuff was always the remedy. Even good dads had a hard time denying them.

Millennials are still known as the selfish generation. It would be nice of we could fix that. It is said that they need to look up the meaning of the word, friend, each time somebody accuses them of being one. They are tarred with being the lazy and entitled generation, because from my observations, they often behave that way. Sometimes I wonder if I am the only one who sees it?

Maybe they have a really valid beef with life. Their generation is saddled with $1.45 billion in student loan debt. That would keep many smiles down. This book is written for the flawless millennials, so they can see their flaws as others see them and know why they have them. It is written for moms and dads and kindergarten teachers and lots of others, hoping that we never put out a group of participation trophy winners like this ever again. This author believes that being a millennial is not a terminal disease and the more the patient knows about herself, the easier the cure will be.

There are better solutions to the problem of millennials as we have come to know them, and many of them are presented in this book. We identify most of the issues and subtly look for solutions. Just like Alcoholics Anonymous and ALANON, and others, we need to come up with a way to have a viable self-help program for millennials. We, the Boomers, in many ways did this to them. Now, we must help them move on to a nice, normal, life.

Why did Brian W. Kelly write this book?

Brian W. Kelly saw the problem of the entitlement mentality of millennials first-hand as a college professor. He wrote this book because he cares about recent college graduates being able to deal with life as it really exists so they can move on with their lives. I am publishing this book because I care. This book identifies the most notable and most serious flaws in the reasons millennials are millennials and it creates plausible arguments for how this does not have to be.

I hope you enjoy this book and I hope that it inspires you to take the individual actions necessary to help the government of the US stand firm against any attacks on democracy from outside or from within this great country. A great start of course is to stop the government's gouging of young Americans, who are plagued with massive government sanctioned student debt. Instead government should be a helpful tool in solving this deep moral dilemma for our country.

Oh, yes, of course, millennials, the generation right before the Z generation, should begin to act like real Americans. If they choose not to, since this is America, other Americans will continue to not be very pleased with them!

I wish you the best.

Brian P. Kelly, Publisher
Wilkes-Barre, Pennsylvania

Table of Contents:

About the Author

Brian W. Kelly retired as an Assistant Professor in the Business Information Technology (BIT) program at Marywood University, where he also served as the IBM i and Midrange Systems Technical Advisor to the IT Faculty. Kelly designed, developed, and taught many college and professional courses. He continues as a contributing technical editor to a number of IT industry magazines, including "The Four Hundred" and "Four Hundred Guru," published by IT Jungle.

Kelly is a former IBM Senior Systems Engineer and IBM Mid Atlantic Area Specialist. His specialty was designing applications for customers as well as implementing advanced IBM operating systems and software facilities on their machines.

He has an active information technology consultancy. He is the author of 163 books and numerous technical articles. Kelly has been a frequent speaker at COMMON, IBM conferences, and other technical conferences.

Brian was a candidate for US Congress from Pennsylvania in 2010 and he brings a lot of experience to his writing endeavors.

Brian Kelly knows the problems caused by the mere notion of millennials and he knows the impact of major issues such as the student debt crisis on the hearts and souls of millennials. Brian has also written books about how to solve the student debt crisis without bankrupting America. The father of three millennials, Brian sees millennials for what they are—and he knows his suggestions in this book can make their lives much better as well of the lives they touch.

Chapter 1 Generations—Boomers, Millennials, X,Y, Z, & Others

MULTIPLE GENERATIONS @ WORK

Five Generations Working Side by Side in 2020

TRADITIONALISTS Born 1900-1945	BOOMERS Born 1946-1964	GEN X Born 1965-1976	MILLENNIAL Born 1977-1997	GEN 2020 After 1997
Great Depression	Vietnam, Moon Landing	Fall of Berlin Wall	9/11 Attacks	Age 15 and Younger
World War II	Civil/Women's Rights	Gulf War	Community Service	Optimistic
Disciplined	Experimental	Independent	Immediacy	High Expectations
Workplace Loyalty	Innovators	Free Agents	Confident, Diversity	Apps
Move to the 'Burbs	Hard Working	Internet, MTV, AIDS	Social Everything	Social Games
Vaccines	Personal Computer	Mobile Phone	Google, Facebook	Tablet Devices

Each generation brings its own view of the world, which creates both opportunities and threats to businesses. This demands Generational Intelligence!

MULTIPLE GENERATIONS @ WORK SURVEY

Since this book is primarily about millennials, before we do anything else let's define a millennial? A millennial is part of a specific generation of births. Generations provide researchers the opportunity to look at Americans both by their place in the life cycle – whether a young adult, a middle-aged parent or a retiree – and by their membership in a cohort of individuals who were born at a similar time.

The Pew Research Center is one of many who study trends in age groups on various issues. They choose to use 1996 as the last birth year for millennials in their analyses. Others go as far as 2002. Thus, anyone born between 1981 and 1996 (ages 22 to 37 in 2018) will be considered a Millennial, and, according to Pew, anyone born from 1997 onward will be part of a new generation.

Since the oldest among this rising generation are just turning 21 this year, and most are still in their teens, the Pew Research Center believes that it is too early to give the "post millennials" a name. But, this does not prevent other groups from naming them.

You will hear terms such as Generation Z or Gen Z (also known as the iGeneration, iGen and Post-Millennials) used to describe the generation after millennials. Most of Generation Z have used the Internet since a young age, and they are generally comfortable with technology and with interacting on social media

Experts suggest that the emphasis on naming generations comes from companies who want to sell something to a specific age group and want a convenient way of referring to a group. We will take a shot at naming all the generations in this chapter.

"Millennial" as a term was coined in the late 1980s by the consultants Neil Howe and William Strauss. Both of these gentlemen are baby boomers and were "boomers" long before the term Generation X was even popularized. (They wanted to call millennials the "13th Gen," but that didn't stick, and neither did "slackers.").

What is a generation?

It is easy to get your mix all talked up in today's crazy world of classifying and labelling generations of human beings based on when they were born. And, so we now have jargon in use today that expects everybody to understand certain phrases such as "Gen X," "Baby Boomer", "The Greatest Generation," etc.

To be able to engage in regular conversation with most people today, it helps Americans to have a reasonably good idea of what these and other generational terms actually mean. Without necessarily knowing a particular generation, most of us at least have an idea as to what comprises a generation. In my day, we used the term generation to refer to a 20-year period in duration, but it means a bit more than that today.

It would be more correct today to say that a generation is a group of people born around the same time and raised around the same place. People in a particular "birth cohort," or generation, often exhibit similar characteristics, preferences, and values over their lifetimes

If somebody says to you, for example, "Oh, that happened three generations ago," how long ago might that be. Fifty years ago, the answer would simply be 20 years times 3 generations equals 60 years. Not today.

We still reckon the passage of time by generations, especially for those indefinite periods measured by a number of successive parent-child relationships. But just how long is a generation? Is it still 20 years?

In recent years, it is a matter of common knowledge that a generation averages about 25 years from the birth of a parent to the birth of a child, even though in specifics, it varies case by case. Yes, admittedly this was closer to 20 years in earlier times when humans mated younger and life expectancies were shorter? In this brief example, we can certainly conclude that the term generation as a term that depicts the passing of time is a moving target that today is somewhere between twenty and twenty-five years and as time goes by, we can expect that to change.

Today, it is not good enough to refer to generations as time periods as most people when discussing generations have a specific starting period and ending period, of which they are interested. And so, we find terms such as "Gen X," "Baby Boomer", "The Greatest Generation, and others to refer to specific generations, all of which represent periods that are in the neighborhood of twenty to twenty-five years in duration, though even this is not a hard rule.

It can be argued that these phrases, used in the lingo of today, come from the larger discipline of demographics, and are used most frequently by market researchers, looking for a theoretically simple, one or two-word phrase to capture the notion of a particular age grouping. Most often such phrases are developed by companies so that sales campaigns can be directed towards specific groups. However, more and more people if not mostly everybody today has begun to use the words for various generations and sub-generations to avoid appearing dumb.

These cue words or phrases for the subcomponents of society are mainly demarcated by age and thus, they are not only useful, but are generally the language used by non-demographers (you and I) and society as a whole when discussing the current spectrum of population cohorts.

Because one cannot just begin talking about millennials without explaining what they are and where they fit, we begin this chapter and this book by providing this primer on the identification and description of the population cohorts in America as currently agreed upon by demographers and market researchers. However, even though most agree, this definition does not mean that this is the one source to which you can go to get the definitions. There are other sources and their definitions may not be exactly fit those shown in this chapter.

Let's start defining generations beginning with the turn of the twentieth century and go to definitions that exist today:

- ✓ Traditionalists or Silent Generation: Born 1945 & before
- ✓ Baby Boomers: Born 1946 to 1965
- ✓ Generation X: Born 1966 to 1976
- ✓ Millennials or Generation Y or Echo Boomers: Born 1977 to 1995
- ✓ Generation Z, iGen, or Centennials: Born 1996 & later

Traditionalists

The traditionalists or as some call them, the silent generation were born before 1945 and are subdivided by some into the following generations:

- Depression Era Born 1912-1921.
- World War II Era Born 1922 to 1927
- Post War Cohort Born 1928 - 1944

Depression Era 1912-1921

Depression era individuals tend to be conservative, compulsive savers, maintain low debt and use more secure financial products like CDs versus stocks. These individuals tend to feel a responsibility to leave a legacy to their children. Tend to be patriotic, oriented toward work before pleasure, respect for authority, have a sense of moral obligation.

World War II 1922-1927

People in this cohort shared in a common goal of defeating the Axis powers. There was an accepted sense of "deferment" among this group, contrasted with the emphasis on "me" in more recent (i.e. Gen X) cohorts.

Post War Cohort 1928-1944

This sub-generation had significant opportunities in jobs and education as the War ended and a post-war economic boom overtook America. However, the growth in Cold War tensions, the potential for nuclear war and other never before seen threats led to levels of discomfort and uncertainty throughout the generation. Members of this group value security, comfort, and familiar, known activities and environments.

Baby Boomers

The Baby Boomers have also been subdivided in some research into the following generations:

- ✓ Boomers I Born 1946 – 1954
- ✓ Boomers II, aka Generation Jones Born 1955 – 1965

Baby Boomers I 1946-1954

For a long time, all Baby Boomers were defined as those born between 1945 and 1964. That would make the generation huge (71 million) and encompass people who were 20 years apart in age.

It did not make sense for those born in 1964 compared with those born in 1946. Life experiences were completely different. Attitudes, behaviors and society were vastly different.

In effect, all the elements that help to define a cohort were violated by the broad span of years originally included in the concept of the Baby Boomers. The first Boomer segment is bounded by the Kennedy and Martin Luther King assassinations, the Civil Rights movements and the Vietnam War. Boomers I were engaged in or they protested the War. Boomers 2 also called the Jones Generation missed the whole thing.

Boomers I had good economic opportunities and were largely optimistic about the potential for America and their own lives, the Vietnam War notwithstanding. The Vietnam War was very unsettling for all Americans but especially the Boomers I cohort.

Baby Boomers 2 1955-1965

This first post-Watergate generation lost much of its trust in government and the mostly optimistic views of the Boomers I generation. Economic struggles including the oil embargo of 1979

The events of the time reinforced a sense of "I'm out for me" and narcissism and a focus on self-help and skepticism over media and institutions. These are representative of attitudes of this cohort.

While Boomers I had Vietnam, Boomers II had AIDS as part of their rite of passage. The youngest members of the Boomer II generation in fact did not have the benefits of the Boomer I class as many of the best jobs, opportunities, housing etc. were taken by the larger and earlier group. Both Gen X and Boomer II folks suffer from this long shadow of opportunity lost by Boomers I.

Generation X 1966-1976

Sometimes referred to as the "lost" generation, this was the first generation of "latchkey" kids, exposed to lots of daycare and divorce. They are one generation removed from the Me-first generation. They are well known as the generation with the lowest voting participation rate of any generation ever.

Gen Xers were quoted by Newsweek as "the generation that dropped out without ever turning on the news or tuning in to the social issues around them." I know when we got an X-Genner at IBM, they were not thankful like we were to work for such a great company but instead were looking for something from the company without providing much in return.

Gen X is often characterized by high levels of skepticism, "what's in it for me" attitudes and a reputation for some of the worst music to ever gain popularity.

Now, moving into adulthood William Morrow (Generations) cited the childhood divorce of many Gen Xers as "one of the most decisive experiences influencing how Gen Xers will shape their own families". Gen Xers are arguably the best educated generation with 29% obtaining a bachelor's degree or higher (6% higher than the previous cohort).

And, with that education and a growing maturity, they are forming families with a higher level of caution and pragmatism than their parents demonstrated. Concerns run high over avoiding broken homes, kids growing up without a parent around and financial planning.

Generation Y, Echo Boomers or Millenniums 1977-1995

The largest cohort since the Baby Boomers, their high numbers reflect their births as that of their parent generation. The last of the Boomer I's and most of the Boomer II's. Gen Y kids are known as incredibly sophisticated, technology wise, immune to most traditional marketing and sales pitches…as they not only grew up with it all, they've seen it all and been exposed to it all since early childhood.

Gen Y members are much more racially and ethnically diverse and they are much more segmented as an audience aided by the rapid expansion in Cable TV channels, satellite radio, the Internet, e-zines, etc.

Gen Y are less brand loyal, and the speed of the Internet has led the cohort to be similarly flexible and changing in its fashion, style consciousness and where and how it communicates.

Gen Y kids often raised in dual income or single parent families have been more involved in family purchases…everything from groceries to new cars. One in nine Gen Yers has a credit card co-signed by a parent.

Generation Z 1996 and later

The Generation Z cohort have just begun to become young adults in recent years. We know a lot about the environment in which they grew up. This highly diverse environment is making the grade schools of the last defined generation the most diverse ever.

Higher levels of technology are making significant inroads in academics allowing for customized instruction, data mining of student histories to enable pinpoint diagnostics and remediation or accelerated achievement opportunities.

Gen Z kids are growing up with a highly sophisticated media and computer environment and are more Internet savvy and expert than their Gen Y, millennial forerunners. But, Millennials never admit not knowing anything about anything so we would never know from listening to them.

The end of the Millennial generation and the start of Gen Z in the United States are closely tied to September 11, 2001. That day marks the number-one generation-defining moment for Millennials. Members of Gen Z—born in 1996 and after—cannot process the significance of 9/11 and it's always been a part of history for them. The research continues on all generations but Gen Z is just out the shoot so we will be getting even more interesting findings as time goes by.

Chapter 2 What is Really Wrong with Young Americans

The millennial trick: only care about oneself

Young Americans are often lumped together under the term "millennials." One of the raps that stick on millennials is that they care about nobody but themselves and they are creating a new world order in which nobody cares about them. It is the ultimate karma. So far, it sure appears they deserve the rap.

As a group, they ought to be ashamed of themselves; but they will never admit shame. They know everything. Instead of reflection, they dig in against the thought of themselves not being perfect, while clutching their T-Ball participation trophy close to their hearts. The trophy is symbolic of the good-old days when simply breathing normally could bring a big participation award. As they reach adulthood, millennials become very disturbed about a new three-letter concept that they must endure that makes getting older not worth it –> J-O-B

These new Americans come in many shapes and sizes. Most can be recognized by their disrespect for their flag, their country, and their elders. They are empowered by the feelings they receive from those emotions. They feel that they have a right to everything anybody else possesses. After all, who else might be more deserving?

Compared with the world

An international study found America's millennials are lacking in major job skills areas such as literacy, problem solving, and job skills. This is a problem that participation trophies cannot help correct. And, that is why the proverbial problem with millennials will take a while to fix.

There is major irony in the discovery of this problem as there is no doubt that US millennials especially are the most educated and tech savvy generation of all in the U.S. Yet, millennials in the US, according to this study, are the world's least skilled people. That hurts but most Americans, especially Boomers, are aware there is some problem with millennials.

We are talking about a recent study by the Educational Testing Service (ETS) that demonstrates conclusively that America's millennials, on average, display weak skills in literacy, math and problem solving when compared to international competition. The study examined millennials from 22 countries, including the United States. It was part of the International Assessment of Adult Competencies Program.

The authors reported that the average scores for U.S. millennials were lower than in many other countries and that the U.S. ranked at the bottom in numeracy and PS-TRE. By the way, PS-TRE is defined as: "using digital technology, communication tools, and networks to acquire and evaluate information, communicate with others, and perform practical tasks. Considering it is a rare moment that millennials are seen without some digital device, the PS-TRE rating is very unexpected. I suspect the problem here is not understanding digital technology but communication.

The U.S. ranked first in just one area: In the study, it had the widest gap of any of the countries between the achievement of those in the top 10 percent and those in the bottom 10 percent of performance.

Seventy-two percent of young adults with a high school diploma or less did not meet minimum proficiency levels in numeracy. In fact, the top performing millennials in the U.S. scored lower than top-performing millennials in 15 of the 22 participating countries. Experts have thus concluded that this means that the US skills challenge is systemic.

Low-scoring U.S. millennials ranked last and scored lower than their peers in 19 participating countries. My personal analysis concludes that if there were not so many documented issues already with millennials in the US, experts would be taking issue with the validity of the testing and its possible bias towards the US in one way or another. The problem for America is that these test results are believable.

Millennials, Democracy & other American notions

As reported in The New York Times, one of the Young American's favorite rag, millennials, in particular, appear to be turning their backs on democracy. No kidding! Lots of things that my generation would simply dismiss is now the gospel understood by the younger generation.

The Baby Boomers' distaste for the lying Grey Lady has not reached our younger Americans who would give up Democracy in a heartbeat as they believe that army rule would be either "good" or "very good for the country." This statistic for those long in the tooth that is a planned bequeath to millennials rose to 1 in 6 in 2014. Compare this with 1 in 16 in 1995.

Whereas 43 percent of older Americans believe it is wrong for a military to take over even if government performs incompetently, only 19 percent of young Americans agreed. Millennials compared with the 60's generation are a definite anomaly.

They love the fake news media to pieces. They love believing lies and arguing points ad absurdum. They love liberal progressive coffee-breath professors who get them involved in great American activities such as protesting free speech and such. Isn't America great?

Millennials love the Democratic Party sometimes, but only the Bern factions, for providing them with encouragement through petty participation activities and trophies. Some are fully dedicated to gaining a lifetime participation trophy in the art of participation. However, few can make decisions and, so they have yet to choose an endeavor in which they wish to be recognized as participatory.

As some are beginning the aging process, though they won't admit it, they are pleased that the magazines on the rack at Dr. Bosley's (The Hair Guy) Office never show anything negative about life. More than ever, these young Americans as they progress in years find, themselves like us all, getting a little thin on the hair and thin on the tooth as they become long in the tooth. It's just as it is. They continue nonetheless to believe they need nothing that older generations needed because they are invincible.

Out of necessity, those who as undergraduates, took their coffee-breath professor's opinions to heart, have found that participation at free events such as the Soup Kitchens across America provides not only a new kind of rush, but they have found the experience is also very nourishing at the right price—free!

Despite how they measure their gains in life, they do wonder why anybody would give up a fun day in the sun or snow to work in such a kitchen; but the food is so darn good, they can't help coming back for more. They never give a thought as to where the food comes from as they have better things to think about such as their collective hate for the President.

We can bet they'll soon be standing in line if they begin to give out trophies for participation in anti-Trump rallies. It would be just like getting a participation trophy in the youth soccer league for the year in which they could not play because they were sick.

From my personal observations as they grow older, these young Americans, aka millennials, might even consider joining in on anti-American rallies if the promoters promised everybody the coveted participation trophies. Wow! Isn't life great!

Blame mom and dad first

Children do not reach the age of reason until seven years old, or so, we are told. So, we certainly cannot blame the diaper boy or the potty girl and that gets us to three or four, just about the age of competitive sports—and the still recent phenomenon, participation trophies.

So, at least until they were seven, millennials were not the biggest problem in their probable future demise. It was mom and dad for sure.

Since I have used this term a number of times in this book, let's find a definition for participation trophy. You probably already guessed it. Here is a definition from Wikipedia: "A participation trophy is a trophy given to children who participate in a sporting event but do not finish in first, second or third place, and so would not normally be eligible for a trophy. It is frequently associated with millennials."

There are a lot of moms and dads of theirs (the young American millennials) who have sucked up every word that ultra-lib Rachel Maddow and her ilk have ever uttered. Looking around at their flawless junior and/or juniorettes, you can get a feeling about all the good the participation trophies really did for their families.

Moms and dads are ultimately responsible for junior and juniorette. I know my parents would leave the blame right there where it belongs. However, my mom and dad did not have to do so because they were their kids' teachers all our lives. I never wanted to cross my mom or dad, for example, because I loved them, and I respected them. They were part of that special generation and they worked hard to make sure the five siblings in my family were all OK. They also reached out and helped others.

Writing for AARP, The Magazine in 2016, Sally Koslow and Caity Weaver net it out quickly about "The Terrible 22's. I love the title:

Sorry, kids: we made you this way

"It's become a weary trope: Millennials, we are often told, are a pampered cohort sulking in their childhood bedrooms or aimlessly couch surfing in search of personal fulfillment. It's easy to get all judgy about the terrible 22s. But that's just part of the problem. What's truly terrible isn't our kids — it's us, the hyper-attentive parents who made them. Consider the oft-quoted profundity that parents should give children both roots and wings. We seem to have neglected *part two*.

...

"This generation is less able to perform in a tough world because of their high expectations about how easy things will be," says Jean Twenge, author of *Generation Me: Why Today's Young Americans Are More Confident, Assertive, Entitled — and More Miserable Than Ever Before.* We've put our children on a pedestal and given lots of praise without having rules. After such a childhood, reality hits like a smack in the face."

"Some parents never bothered to teach everyday life skills and assumed the role of concierge /personal assistant. We did this on purpose, says Mary Dell Harrington of the parenting blog Grown and Flown: "Taking care of practical things — making doctors' appointments or buying gifts for family members—becomes a sneaky way for parents to maintain codependence." Our logic: If our kids manage well without us, that must mean we are old."

That is an indictment of millennial parents if I have ever read one. Thank you Sally, Caty, and the others.

The school district is not responsible for anybody's kids once they leave mom and dad. The parents are responsible. Great Kindergarten training can help; but great parents hold the keys to their children's future more than anybody else. I get the idea that moms and dad's worried about careers more than kids got us into the millennial caricature mess. Is it a caricature or is it reality is what is yet to be determined?

Unfortunately, today, even I, as a nationalist, populist, Trump-loving conservative, have no choice but to admit that there are many co-conspirators to the demise of American youth. Thus, what has happened to our young Americans cannot be dismissed as simple circumstance, or a death wish of the young. At the very least we know something went terribly wrong with a whole generation of Americans. We see it every day.

How about if we explore all these notions further. Let's review how our millennial young Americans have been left to form their negative opinions of America and their fellow Americans. Let's summarize a look from the time before they become young adults until the time they graduate from their college or university.

✓ 1 Moms and Dads who love liberalism and progressivism and socialism, forgot all their lessons and so all the juniors never had a chance.

✓ 2. Liberal / progressive coffee breath professors in universities have no shame nor love of truth.

✓ 3. Fake news from the finest liars in the universe seems real.

✓ 4. Democrats rooting against the good things in America can be convincing if they offer participation rewards.

✓ 5. Socialist / progressives who hate US Capitalism are on the liberal fake news channel all day long.

How my dad would have handled it.

My dad ruled our home with an iron fist. His Motto was "my wife is the master of this house…whatever she shall say shall be done." I can recall the thing in my life that made all else seem better. With a loving mom and grandmom, and a father that took no crap, my brothers and I got real lessons in life and my sisters got a lot of love. There were no spankings for my two sisters, who today, we call the *Dolly Sisters*.

Here is a composite story of what it was like to have done something wrong in our home as a boy, and the sheer agony of waiting for my father to get home to mete out the required punishment. This was such an ordeal, let me assure you all, the offenses were few and far between and unlike millennials of today, the lesson was well learned.

"When I had done something so bad that my mother would say those most feared words, "Wait 'til your father gets home, young man," I knew I was in real trouble. When my punishment was over, I felt better. I think most millennials never saw the almost knockout punch of a father nor the sting of a thick belt on the butt. Both remedies had a way of correcting problems with my dad's kids in a lasting way.

My springboard to safety as a real young kid was my grandmother, who I loved to pieces. So, when I would get one of those cautions from my mom, I would go to grand mom. My hard-of-hearing grandmother, the sweetest lady in the world, would see it differently in my favor. Maybe! When I went and pleaded my case, if grand mom's hearing problem came into play, however, and she offered no consolation, I knew my goose was cooked.

When my father got home, he hated his supper to be interrupted, but I would hear my mother making the case about me. In minutes, dad was from the kitchen table, calling my name. I tried to hide a lot of times, but it was always worse when I reappeared, so I came to him and the first thing he would say is: "Get to bed!"

That was tough punishment enough but that was not the end of it. It was not even 4:00 in the afternoon and that was it – no radio, no B/W TV—nothing for a whole night. Sometimes even my cat, Pouter Pootman would not even show up. Worse than that, I knew it was not over because dad had to eat and take his bath and the bath was upstairs right by where I was.

If the offense was especially egregious, after saying "Get to Bed," my father would call me over and recite the offenses that I had perpetrated and then he would say something scary. Then he would take his right arm and hold it high, so I could see his huge fist, and he would begin to swing it at me like a knock-out punch. Right before it hit my nose, he would put his left hand in front of it to catch it. I would hear the thud of his two-hands, but no pain. He never used his hands on me— ever.

Then I ran like a little bugger up the steps, while he was eating supper. When he came up, I was never sure what was next. But, if I saw him take his belt off, he was like Paladin, San Francisco. Paladin never took out his gun unless he planned to use it. Dad never removed his belt unless he planned to use it. I knew what was coming.

I knew that I was the reason he took the belt off, and I ran like heck. He would track me down, typically under one of the beds, and again, hiding never made it better. Then I would get a few whacks on the butt with the belt. He never doubled it up so it was as long as forever and part of it always hit me and it stung.

Then, it would be over, and he would chastise me again to be good. Following this, he went downstairs to watch TV with the non-perpetrators in the family. I of course was in bed for the evening and it was not even 5:00 PM. I had a lot to think about in terms of how I got into the mess, and I always did. I never wanted such medicine again.

I fear that many millennials never had one session such as that or they would have changed their evil ways. I know that I did. It was a combination of love and fear.

One of my recent books requested that Congress and our new president solve the millennial crisis, which in that book was about all of the student debt that they owed. It is truly a sin that Congress by its action and inaction has cut a 20-year hole in American History. They have taken away many of the opportunities that would make millennials real people.

Young Americans, mostly millennials, suffered through a combination of bad parenting, short-lasting Kindergarten lessons, and a penchant for the liberal side. It has gotten worse. They are now literally choking on their student debt. Most should never have taken the loans. Nonetheless, the staggering student debt has their lives stopped. Studying the matter, the responsibility for this is directly related to a Congress that is not doing its job. Check out this book

https://www.amazon.com/dp/1947402234
Wipe Out All Student Loan Debt--Now!: Unique solutions to the $1.45 Trillion debt accumulation

Each year that this problem is not solved by Congress, is another year for many millennials in a veritable debtor's prison. It is so bad that 50% in a recent survey would be willing to give up their most fundamental freedom, the right to vote, to have their debt lifted and be able to lead a normal life. I do feel sorry for millennials in a lot of ways

Bruce Ritter, writing for The RealTruth.com discusses the rise of the millennials. Without even writing a word in the piece, Ritter captures the essence of the millennial in his subtitle: *Why They Know So Much…Yet Understand So Little.* Ritter notes:

" They are smart, resourceful, talented, highly educated, team-oriented and well-traveled. Yet the average Millennial does not know how to professionally conduct him or herself in the office. He lacks the training to use proper etiquette at business dinners and other special occasions. He was not taught to value the hands-on experience of older, more seasoned generations. And he does not know how and when to accept "no" for an answer."

Ritter sees some of these lifetime events as contributing factors that millennials have had to overcome. Consider the life-defining events that shaped their young lives:

- The Columbine shooting
- The 9/11 attacks
- Corporate corruption scandals
- War on Terrorism
- Anti-Americanism
- A nuclear North Korea
- Emerging nations
- The "dot-com boom"
- Pocket Electronics
- Hurricane Katrina
- Lots of others

With all of this baggage, millennials are not being excused by the world. They are cocky and pompous and many seem lazy. They look like they walk like they own the world.

They know it all from all the parenting and life guidance mistakes to which they were subjected. Yet, they feel no need for correction, and that is their biggest problem today. There is no fix for anyone unwilling to listen to the fix. They need a special treatment like AA to get them out of their funk or they will be the missing generation in US history.

Nobody was ever able to tell them what to do and so they never saw a need to listen and they still do not listen. Even today, when they are hurting, they place the blame in the wrong places and they cling to liberal progressive and hateful ideals that are more harmful that the poor lessons of their early lives.

For Boomers, the millennials of today serve the same role as President Trump does for Never-Trumpers. There has to be somebody that we can set up as the bad guy. Millennials are not that bad and should not be punished by America, but then again, neither should President Trump. When we fix that part of our culture, we will all be better off. Perhaps we will all, with the help of millennials who are in many ways are MIA, we will be able to reclaim an entire generation of human beings. Let's hope we can.

No, we should not deport them, but sometimes they make us feel like we would if we could.

Chapter 3 Life Lessons for Millennials from Kindergarten

Kindergarten helps children all over the world

The term "KinderGarten" originated in Germany yet the notion has served many countries as the first step to helping children become adults. Froebel called for German women to come together and support the kindergarten. Because he described children as plants and teachers as gardeners, the term kindergarten emerged—kinder meaning child, and garten—meaning garden.

There comes a time when all parents must be ready to send their little ones to Kindergarten. Some send the kids out to a short half-day of pre-school for a few years for developing social skills, even before Kindergarten, while others may choose to wait an extra year to send their young ones to "K" so that the home studies are not negated by the "rowdiness" formal classroom setting.

Millennials and what happened to them in this generation is the topic of study in this book. Deportation would work but we can do better.

Many like me think that more than a few lessons at home and more than a few Kindergarten lessons are not in the repertoire of today's young Americans, for which we in the older generations, believe they suffer. It may not be their fault, but recent observations of their behavior suggest that they make it no better for themselves than if it were.

Let's look at some of the preparatory things that would help your child, or my child, in life especially before they even arrive at Kindergarten. Chances are the bulk of millennials today would have grown up to be much better people with some of these tips.

MILLENNIALS...

THE GENERATION THAT REACHED THEIR PEAK WHEN THEY GRADUATED FROM KINDERGARTEN.

imgflip.com

Kindergarten teachers are certified in knowing everything

I think from reading what they have written that I would agree they know more than most of us about how to have a wonderful life.

Kindergarten teachers love their new classes every year. Like any good teacher, they would love students to show up with all of the basic skills they need for sure. Some of these skills are very helpful at tender ages than others. None of the pre-skills are mandatory, but the five items we discuss below would help if a child knew them before beginning Kindergarten.

Parents in many "K" books are urged to help their little ones prepare for Kindergarten by helping prepare them for life.

Not all of us have the benefit of having a Kindergarten teacher right next door but Kindergarten teachers do love to write. And, so their great musings are posted all over the Internet. You can therefore check on my tips with impunity if you care to do so.

The things I discuss may seem little to you, or not-important, but Kindergarten teachers believe they are HUGE. Why? They give your child confidence as they show the teacher that your child is independent and more than ready to take on Kindergarten!

K-Teachers like to see the little things because it is the little things that give your child that feeling of success and leadership. Though not all children will be destined for everybody's definition of success and not all will be prepared for leadership, getting it right in the beginning gives every child an edge on all of those children of parents who let it ride.

I wish I had developed this list of five things by myself as I am a proud dad who, along with a great mom, a great mother, sent three little ones to Pre-School and eventually off to Kindergarten as hard as it was to part with the little tykes, especially the first day. I was always there, and it took my heart away watching the little guys' movements from the playpen to organized social constructs.

The 5 items on my list can be found in a February 2017 book titled Getting Ready for Kindergarten. The book by Becky Mansfield and Jenae Jacobson is designed to show you what your child should know before Kindergarten. Unfortunately, at the time of this writing, there is no proof that a SPECIAL "K" class would help today's millennials become better people, though I bet that a thorough reading of this book might.

Let me repeat my introduction—not all of us have the benefit of having a Kindergarten teacher right next door but Kindergarten teachers do love to write, and therefore, their great stuff is posted all over the Internet. So, of course you can check on my tips if you care to do so.

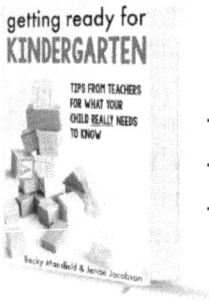

getting ready for
KINDERGARTEN
TIPS FROM TEACHERS FOR WHAT YOUR CHILD REALLY NEEDS TO KNOW

Becky Mansfield & Jenae Jacobson

is your child ready for kindergarten?

$9.99 limited time price

Here is the list. It would help millenniels, I do believe, but I am more inclined to believe that this generation needs a redo on the whole idea of Kindergarten.

Here is what a real pre-Kindergartner should know before that first day in the big "K" classroom.

1. Tie their shoes.

There is a whole process and every step counts. Children must practice the exercise at home in steps. First, for a few days, teach them to do the X and go through the first loop. This is the easiest part. Like everything with a child, this becomes learned by doing it over and over. Let them tie everything (cushions on chairs, your shoes, aprons, etc. When your child is seventeen, perhaps they can learn how to tie their coffee-breath professor's handlebar mustache or the strands of his beard. OK, maybe by then, it is too late for a rescue for that.

Next, move onto the rest of the tying process as shown in this great book cited above.

2. Open a juice box.

It is OK if you do not appease your child at home with little juice boxes. This exercise is helpful as an equalizer even if your child drinks water with their lunch. They will encounter parties and celebrations in schools in which juice boxes are the norm.

These happen more & more often these days. Teachers will open the juice boxes they provide if the children cannot open them. Birthdays happen quite often in a classroom with 20+ children. Teach them at home to open a juice box step by step just like tying shoes. Take the straw off, open it, insert it into the juice box, drink it, throw it all away.

Know that there are too many 5 and 6-year-olds that do not do this because no one has taught them how. Four and five-year old's love to open their own juice boxes at parties and it makes them feel like such a "big kid." Feeling like a big kid is OK! —when you are a little kid, especially.

3. Use the bathroom, wash hands and button pants alone.

This is a big one, but it is easy too—with patience. As a point of note, if your child cannot button their pants without help, until they learn, please send them in different pants until they master pants. You can bet most kids do not want to walk out, in front of 20 fellow-students, to ask the teacher to button their pants. Like all worthwhile pre-K tasks, practice, practice, practice, to avoid your child being embarrassed. Make sure your child knows that when embarrassed about anything, they should discuss the issue with parents.

4. How to handle getting what they need.

This may not be obvious; but it is about helping your child to take responsibility for themselves in previously unrehearsed areas. For example, think about your child breaking their pencil in class. Then what? Will they know that they should raise their hand to get another one?

Your child will not want to sit there, doing nothing, simply because one of the five items we are covering now was not what just happened to them.

They need to know that it is their job to take care of themselves. Think of a child not eating his yogurt for lunch because mom did not pack a spoon. Mom wisely would ask the young student: "Don't they have spoons there?" It may take a while for a student to get what she is saying but if she explained it well if she did not pack him a spoon (or napkin or a straw), she could tell him that he needs to get up, get in line, and take care of his needs.

The moral of course is that these things happen all the time in all settings in which children are not with parents, and no one is going to do it for him. The objective all along is to raise a child to be a responsible adult. There are those of us out here that can already see that today's young Americans missed many of these great lessons. We would all appreciate that moms and dads and "K" teachers can help us for sure.

5. Know the basics!

There is lots to know for four and five-year-olds scared in their boots about moving forward in life. Feel free to work on any of these exercises well before Kindergarten.

The major questions and concerns are: Does your child know their own name, phone number, and address? Knowing these are very important! Think about a teacher with twenty to twenty-five dependent miniature people who are her / his students for the day.

What about the other 24 students? Can you rely on any teacher always having time for your child?

While sure that the kids will be safe, parents would not want to send their little ones out 'into the world' without this needed information. Hard as it is to believe, it helps to add LAST NAME to the above list too, not just their first.

If your last name is long such as Sniptaggerinom, and it is hard to spell or remember, another great suggestion is at least to slip a piece of paper in between their sock & their shoe with the info on it.

This is what a number of parents do, not just at school, but when they go out somewhere with a lot of other people, like an amusement park Chances are your "lost child," God forbid, will be found much sooner when they know how to find their information slip. So, the kids need to know to look for the slip there, in case they "forget" the specifics of the Sniptaggerinom surname.

Most parents want to be good parents but not everybody can know everything. Hopefully, you can see how important these five points would be in assuring that a child could be independent and safe even before Kindergarten.

Unfortunately, when your children grow up and go to college, they will meet what I call "coffee-breath professors" of both genders who know it all. Let me offer another way to handle these "know it all's."

Before your recent HS graduates go to get their higher education, you can help them to not be affected by the negative spew that in recent years we have seen coming out of those who are supposed revered professors. The coffee-breaths of these professors give them away.

Not all millennials are the caricatures of millennials that we find today in most people's minds. Those with good parents and good life principles have the most chance for success.

We can breathe a sigh of relief as we just worked our way through the Pre-"K" Lesson. There are lots of great lessons taught in Kindergarten itself. There are many books written about the Kindergarten time of a child's life and about how important Kindergarten lessons are to the rest of life.

As we can see by the problems young Americans are having coping with life in America today, not everybody picked up life's lessons on Kindergarten. It is amazing how many young Americans still don't get it. It is as if they never went to Kindergarten.

The best Kindergarten book of all time

The world recognized best book on Kindergarten is titled: *All I Really Need to Know I Learned in Kindergarten* by <u>Robert Fulghum</u>. It is available at all fine book-stores including my distributor, Amazon. Fulghum identifies a number of common principles that are most often taught in Kindergarten. These principles are intended to guide all of us through our lives from getting through childhood to becoming accomplished well-acclimated adults.

In his bestselling book, he amplifies the list with a number of insightful essays. There are a lot of lessons to be learned, especially for those such as many of today's young Americans who did not pay enough attention in Kindergarten

Twenty-five years ago, Robert Fulghum published a simple credo-- a credo that became the phenomenal #1 "New York Times" bestseller "All I Really Need to Know I Learned in Kindergarten." Now, seven million copies later, in his most current edition, Fulghum has written a new preface and twenty-five new essays, adding even more potency to a common, though no less relevant, piece of wisdom: that the most basic aspects of life bear its most important opportunities.

In this new version, Fulghum engages us again with musings on life, death, love, pain, joy, sorrow, and the best chicken-fried steak in the continental U.S.A. The little seed in the Styrofoam cup offers a reminder about our own mortality and the delicate nature of life.

There is lots more to hold our interest such as a spider who catches (and loses) a full-grown woman in its web one fine morning teaching us about surviving catastrophe . . . the love story of Jean-Francois Pilatre and his hot air balloon reminds us to be brave and unafraid to "fly" . . . life lessons hidden in the laundry pile . . . magical qualities found in a box of crayons . . . hide-and-seek vs. sardines--and how these games relate to the nature of God.

All I Really Need to Know I Learned in Kindergarten in its new makeover, continues to brim with the very stuff of life and the significance found in the smallest details.

In the years that have passed since the first publication of this book that touched so many with its simple, profound wisdom, Robert Fulghum has had some time to ponder, to reevaluate, and to reconsider. And in his new book edition, he delivers fresh thoughts on classic topics, right alongside the wonderful new essays.

Perhaps in today's chaotic, more challenging world, these essays on life will resonate even deeper--as readers discover how universal insights can be found in ordinary events. Perhaps if we look deep enough we can find a cure for the procrastinating millennial, who still can't get twenty years after Kindergarten.

Then, again, perhaps Mr. Fulghum has this new breed of cat figured out and the problem is already solved. Boy, would that not be great.

Here are some things shown across the Internet in the many introductions, reviews, and analyses of Fulgham's book.

"I believe that imagination is stronger than knowledge. That myth is more potent than history. That dreams are more powerful than facts. That hope always triumphs over experience. That laughter is the only cure for grief. And I believe that love is stronger than death."
— **Robert Fulghum, All I Really Need to Know I Learned in Kindergarten: Uncommon Thoughts On Common Things**

"These are the things I learned (in Kindergarten):

1. Share everything.
2. Play fair.
3. Don't hit people.
4. Put things back where you found them.
5. CLEAN UP YOUR OWN MESS.
6. Don't take things that aren't yours.
7. Say you're SORRY when you HURT somebody.
8. Wash your hands before you eat.
9. Flush.
10. Warm cookies and cold milk are good for you.
11. Live a balanced life - learn some and drink some and draw some and paint some and sing and dance and play and work every day some.
12. Take a nap every afternoon.
13. When you go out into the world, watch out for traffic, hold hands, and stick together.
14. Be aware of wonder. Remember the little seed in the Styrofoam cup: The roots go down and the plant goes up and nobody really knows how or why, but we are all like that.
15. Goldfish and hamster and white mice and even the little seed in the Styrofoam cup - they all die. So, do we.
16. And then remember the Dick-and-Jane books and the first word you learned - the biggest word of all - LOOK."
— **Robert Fulghum, All I Really Need to Know I Learned in Kindergarten**

"You may never have proof of your importance, but you are more important than you think. There are always those who couldn't do without you. The rub is that you don't always know who."
— **Robert Fulghum, All I Really Need to Know I Learned in Kindergarten**

"Hide-and-seek, grown-up style. Wanting to hide. Needing to be sought. Confused about being found."
— **Robert Fulghum, All I Really Need to Know I Learned in Kindergarten: Uncommon Thoughts on Common Things**

"It's harder to talk about, but what I really, really, really want for Christmas is just this: I want to be 5 years old again for an hour. I want to laugh a lot and cry a lot. I want to be picked or rocked to sleep in someone's arms, and carried up to be just one more time. I know what I really want for Christmas: I want my childhood back. People who think good thoughts give good gifts."
— **Robert Fulghum, All I Really Need to Know I Learned in Kindergarten**

"It doesn't matter what you say you believe - it only matters what you do."
— **Robert Fulghum, All I Really Need to Know I Learned in Kindergarten**

"Every person passing through this life will unknowingly leave something and take something away. Most of this "something" cannot be seen or heard or numbered or scientifically detected or counted. It's what we leave in the minds of other people and what they leave in ours. Memory. The census doesn't count it. Nothing counts without it."
— **Robert Fulghum, All I Really Need to Know I Learned in Kindergarten**

"Think what a better world it would be if we all-the whole world-had cookies and milk about three o'clock every afternoon and then lay down with our blankies for a nap. Or if all governments had as a basic policy to always put things back where they found them and to clean up their own mess.

And it is still true, no matter how old you are-when you go out into the world, it is best to hold hands and stick together."

— **Robert Fulghum, All I Really Need to Know I Learned in Kindergarten**

"Sticks and stones may break our bones, but words will break our hearts"

— **Robert Fulghum, All I Really Need to Know I Learned in Kindergarten**

Kindergarten lessons from the Hallmark Channel

Our lessons from Kindergarten at one time could have come directly from the Hallmark Channel

Even Hallmark Corporation unfortunately, has made some gross errors in its existence. I am hoping for a do-over from a recent decision in which Hallmark left its US employees behind and moved many operations out of the country.

Though they still manage to come through with their fantastic heart-lift with their magical Christmas Specials, they showed recently that it is tough to be a great citizen all of the time. All the great PR in the world cannot make up for how a company behaves behind closed doors.

Locals are asking how Kansas City's famous card making family banked about $4.4 billion in revenue last year if things are so bad. The locals had to give up hundreds of jobs to overseas workers. Some say the company chose to send the hometown jobs to

China. When I heard about it, I asked "Could that really be America's Hallmark?"

My wife is continually impressed with their magical, heart-warming portrayals of life as it should be lived. So it actually would be a values betrayal to find that Hallmark does not live as it preaches that we live. Like my wife, I am in love with Hallmark's Christmas presentations as is the rest of America, but it is unsettling that the company and the Hall family in particular seems to have put greed over goodness.

I hope I am wrong. I include this sidebar in this book so that all Hallmark fans have a chance to write the company to tell them to get back to their basic beliefs.

My skepticism on American business, begins and ends with how American a company chooses to be. Let's let Hallmark explain its "why?" to America in one of its heart-rendering Christmas shows. Hopefully the wrinkle the company spins will be believable. This is what I got about the facts from my research. It is clearly a secret, well-planned betrayal of a town and a country by a company and a family with more prestige to lose than most families could hope to have gained in a lifetime. Here's how the local announcement went:

By the end of the presentation [to the employees] at Hallmark, Manager Lee Burner had revealed the real point of his speech. The artists in the Production Art Division at Hallmark would no longer be working on art. The creative portions of their jobs would disappear.

No longer would they be working on the designs of cards, party supplies or novelty items. Now they'd be called "print production technicians," and instead of designing artwork, they would only be checking to make sure that outsourced artwork was ready for printing. At least at the time, they were not becoming unemployed. I guess even Hallmark cannot be good all the time.

We all need good lessons in life in order to really know how good we should be. Most of these irreplaceable lifetime lessons come from Kindergarten. Those without a great human being as a teacher in Kindergarten may never rise to be as good as they can be.

Of course, much of the work to helping mold a fine person happens right at home. Our parents help us with all of our early lessons, which in a great kindergarten are reinforced and brought to life.

The Hallmark channel is my wife's favorite TV channel. In the summer, she watches their wedding series. Yes, we finally have a colored TV (just kidding). Pat loves Hallmark all the time but especially at Christmas time. I see the glow in her eyes as one good deed follows one good person after another until the Hallmark story plot is complete; the bad guys are thwarted; and the good guys always prove that besides the North Pole, Santa Clause lives in the heart.

What a wonderful lift as this particular channel makes it so easy for all viewers to become immersed in a story that always has a subtle positive feel-good lesson. After a few roller coaster emotional rides, the story always brings the viewer back to a good, safe place in accord with solid Kindergarten values.

Hallmark's skilled writers have a unique way of forcing full grown adults, young, and old, to go back through those great Kindergarten lessons. We can reevaluate ourselves against those great early suggestions such as those from Robert Fulghum, for how to lead our lives. Hallmark puts those Kindergarten lessons to life in its shows but unfortunately, it appears that it does not do so in its own corporate life.

I was convinced that if I searched Hallmark's Corporate Directory, I would find that a brash know-it-all, selfish, millennial grandchild had taken over the company. I figured I would read that some coffee-breath liberal professor had convinced the new millennial CEO that neither Kansas City nor America were important any longer.

With President Donald Trump trying to do his best to make America great again, I surely did not expect what I thought was an America-First company--Hallmark to be fighting Trump's America First Credo.

Donald J. Hall, Jr. is not a millennial and he should know better but apparently, he does not. He runs the company with his brother David. He serves as the chief executive officer of Kansas City, Mo.-based Hallmark Cards, Inc. He also is vice chairman of the Hallmark board of directors and serves on the boards of directors for Crown Media Holdings, Inc., and Hallmark International.

Hall is the grandson of company founder Joyce C. Hall, joined Hallmark in 1971, he has worked in manufacturing, customer service, product development, and sales. He has served as a member of Hallmark's board of directors since 1990.

Neither Donald nor David Hall are even close to being millennials and they both have a ton of money, so I do not understand greed as a driving force for more profits. The best I can do is offer that they may have been unduly influenced by their own nine children, who seem to be of millennial age. But, I have no facts to support such a conclusion. Something surely went wrong.

However, I find little written about any of this younger generation of adult Halls, so I will not speculate. Sometimes companies begin to care more about profit than people. I hope not. Hallmark IMHO, needs a big pro-American recovery.

In a book that hopes to help millennials regain their true spot in history, a major, major task that we must take one step at a time, I am focusing on Hallmark because the Hall family and the company stepped onto the wrong side of the road. America needs to pray that we get our millennials back for sure. To prove we can do that, let's all work on getting the Hall Family and Hallmark back into the America-First fold. If we can do that, then for sure, we have a great shot in convincing God to help our own millennials.

I am not going to stop watching Hallmark, but I may start buying cards someplace else if the Hall Family keep their hearts closed. I wish the Hall Family the best, but my secret Hallmark wish is that they and their very successful company choose to make a positive American mark on everything they do in the future.

From www.pitch.com:

Outsourcing and job cuts may seem normal for corporate America, but Hallmark founder Joyce Hall created his company with the idea of valuing his employees over all else. Hall protected every employee during hard times — even through the Great Depression — until he retired in 1966. The company mantra, still printed on cards and posters given to employees over the years, promises "That the people of Hallmark are our Company's most valuable resource."

I think it's time Hallmark began to tell the truth again. America is unaware of the quiet movement of jobs from America. Maybe there are millennials influencing deployment decisions. Maybe not! Sure seems like it!

From an outsider perspective, Hallmark, with family assets well over 1 $Trillion, with a good part of it made through the work of dedicated home-towners, seems too willing to turn its back on America and Kansas City while still claiming credit for being a great people company. Only the truth flies with today's new Americans.

I hope these words to Hallmark are not too sharp; but it is what I think. My advice to Hallmark is to either bring the jobs back or get out of town and stay out while America finds a new greeting card company.

Chapter 4 Beware of Coffee-Breath Professors

Universities Poison Mush Brained Young Americans

I have been a professor at multiple colleges since getting my MBA at the tender age of twenty-nine, until recently when I ended my career for now at least, as Assistant Professor at Marywood University in Business Information Technology. For years, I experienced first-hand, the onslaught of the millennial revolution. I regret to say that a number of the students that I observed in my tenure had not paid much attention to those invaluable lessons from Kindergarten. I would add that they made easy prey for the pressure of peers and a very liberal coffee-breath faculty.

I saw the never-ending liberal hogwash that became common on campus as one liberal progressive speaker after another was paraded to the public areas to help sway the student thought process towards the liberal side. My friends on the business faculty, secretly conservative, cautioned me not to make waves about my observations. They warned that the response from the administration might be quite career damaging.

Eventually, in two different colleges, I paid the ultimate price for not going along just to get along. I did my job and was respectful. My political leanings however, did match those of the institutions.

I was not one of those progressive "coffee-breath-professors" in the arts departments who influenced students to not love America. The colleges and universities, where I taught were typical American liberal arts institutions in which the sciences and the business areas were tolerated only to keep enrollments up.

Students also had the deck stacked against them if they made their views known to the wrong groups. Faculty, even faculty with full tenure walked gingerly when they carried a conservative message, knowing that the boom could fall in many different ways.

The #2 Radio Talk Show Host in America, Michael Savage, wrote a book in 2010 titled, *Liberalism Is a Mental Disorder."* Savage offered the cure but unfortunately since 2010, there have been few takers. Liberalism still is a mental disorder and in my years in Academia, I saw it first-hand. Liberals are very hateful and vindictive. They still have not gotten over the fact that their guy for President in 2016 did not win.

When I ran for Congress in 2010 as a Democrat, there was a Republican Club at Marywood University. It was the lone conservative voice on campus. I spoke with the moderator, when I ran for office. His name was Frederick Fagel, a very nice man, and an accomplished and tenured professor of economics.

Fred was very sheepish about provoking any more angst and had settled down or, so it seems after building his web site to show how he really felt about conflicting Marywood University values and policies. He continues to pay the renewal fee to host his web site the site but that is all I know right now. His site, which has not been updated since I left Marywood, can be accessed at

http://marywoodfreespeech.com

Front page looks like image above with following text displayed alongside the picture

"Without free speech no search for truth is possible...no discovery of truth is useful...Better a thousand fold abuse of free speech than denial of free speech. The abuse dies in a day, but the denial slays the life of the people, and entombs the hope of the race." {Charles Bradlaugh - British social reformer 1833-1891}

"Welcome to the website dedicated to free speech at Marywood University. Marywood's current policies and practices are antithetical to the principles of academic freedom. To correct the problems caused by the ambiguous existing policies, our group is urging Marywood to enshrine free speech protections on campus. We want action.

"Please take some time to review the materials on this website to learn more about our history, our proposal, and our on-going efforts in the pursuit of this important policy change. If you are a Marywood student, faculty member, or "alum" likewise troubled by the lack of free speech protections on campus, then join us and help us change it!

As noted, this site was last changed in 2009 and I am betting that it was that no policies changed. I taught my last class there in May. 2011.

I found out what happened to Fred. He crossed somebody at the University, and they got him. It is not nice to be a conservative on a liberal campus. I read about Fred again as I was reviewing my facts for the second printing of this book. I spotted an article: *Tenured Prof Sues Marywood U. for Ignoring Its Own Policies to Fire Him.* It was by Susan Kruth and submitted to FIRE (Thefire.org) on December 23, 2014. Here are the first two paragraphs of her post:

> Frederick Fagal, formerly a tenured professor at Marywood University in Pennsylvania, filed a lawsuit against the university in federal court last week alleging that it suspended him and then terminated his employment without following its own written procedures. [They fired me in 2011 under similar circumstances against their own written procedures.]

> Tensions between Fagal and the university arose in late November 2011, when Fagal had FIRE's Will Creeley speak to his "Introduction to Social Science" course. With the university's permission, Fagal had hung posters advertising Will's presentation around campus. But according to Fagal's complaint (obtained via PACER), university personnel removed most of the posters without notice to Fagal, and without citing any policy explaining these actions.

At least Fred got to put some posters up before they took action. You'll learn more about my travails shortly.

Marywood is not a bad university for sure. But, as a Catholic University, they have chosen not to take the lead in renewing Kindergarten values first. Instead, they promote the liberal progressive lifestyle.

One more example before I continue. Like it or not, Catholic Universities are Catholic. They may choose not to act Catholic but if they choose to be Catholic, then the Catholic Church has influence over them whether they like it or not. Lying is an effective tool used by liberals and I have seen it used effectively at Marywood University personally and in this example.

Scranton Diocese' Bishop Martino from back in 2009 was Bishop of Greater Scranton, PA. He thus had pastoral control of Marywood University, though it seemed like the Bishop's fathering was not appreciated by the University.

The Bishop was concerned about Catholic doctrine regarding abortion and contraceptives and he asked the four universities in his care whether they offered devices of any kind to students on campus.

On April 6, 2009, the four schools, feeling the heat from the Bishop, issued a joint letter to diocesan officials stating that none of the schools or campus health centers offered condoms. "Condoms are not available on our campuses and our student health services and centers do not provide oral and other forms of contraception," wrote the presidents of Marywood University, the University of Scranton, Misericordia University, and King's College. "We are, therefore, confident in assuring you that our health centers practice in ways that respect and do not violate Catholic teaching."

In an edition of the diocesan newspaper, The Catholic Light during this period, the Bishops noted that the response "does not answer [our previous] request for 'documents available, which will indicate policies, procedures or practices authorized by' the schools." The bishops (Dougherty and Martino) cited two "practical examples for their concern."

The Marywood University Web site advised international students to "bring contraceptives and condoms to campus," the bishops stated. Catholic Doctrine is Catholic Doctrine but as many Catholics have found sometimes Universities act as if they are above Catholic Doctrine and they are first Academic Institutions. Bishops Dougherty and Martino gave them little wiggle room.

Does free speech come naturally in campus zones?

Before I leave the notion of free speech, the lack of which on campus is one of the reasons why young college students of today have little opportunity to gain different points of view. It is a big reason why those of millennial age begin to behave as millennials and this behavior stays with them after they graduate or leave college.

Let us again look at the free speech on campus issue before we move on. Andrea Tortora wrote a nice piece on September 29, 2017 highlighting this controversial issue. Part of her thesis had to do with AG Jeff Sessions offering his thoughts at Georgetown on the matter.

Regardless of what we may think of Jeff Sessions as Attorney General, he clearly has little regard for "free speech zones" and he sees their blooming on campuses across the country as the antithesis of democracy. It is like a bad disease.

The AG highlighted the limitations being placed on free speech on university campuses in his speech at Georgetown. Sessions is puzzled as to why anybody would want to negatively affect the exchange of unencumbered ideas. Who wants to be muzzled about the important issues of our times?

Without anybody preaching to a thinking person, it should not take much grey matter to realize that when educational institutions begin to narrow the proper interpretation of the First Amendment, we should all be worried. The founders gave us all freedom of speech and it is hard for some of us past fifty to imagine that anybody in America, including college students and the millennial generation, would stand still and give up a right that empowers all citizens to share their thoughts and opinions in public places (especially those places funded by tax dollars).

Unfortunately, it is not free speech but a way of life that defines today's debate. Since free speech is not fully permitted on campuses in America, the discussions over free speech itself is one that finds few participants. Free speech on American campuses is more than an academic or theoretical issue.

Before Attorney General Jeff Sessions delivered his address (about free speech on college campuses) at Georgetown, students and miserable coffee-breath faculty professors had already set the stage by protesting his appearance. They wanted to use their free speech freely to shut down Sessions' free speech.

They could protest freely because they are liberal progressives. Nobody would dare shut them down. They had to get the message out that Jeff Sessions should have no right to his free speech on their campus. Think about that for a minute. It sure is an upside-down world. How can parents today expect their college graduates to grow right-side-up. Policies on college campuses have help create the infamous caricature of the millennial today. Academic institutions are the problem today, not the solution.

Can you imagine the Attorney General of the US, not a terrorist from a foreign country, who would be accorded full campus privileges, was the object of such hate speech? Knowing that it was perpetrated by students led by more than 30 faculty members, you can almost smell their coffee-breaths and their ideology stained mustaches, beards, and lips. What do they know?

Nonetheless, they released a "bold" **statement**, condemning "the [supposed] hypocrisy of Attorney General Sessions speaking about free speech." I ask the readers to consider who the real hypocrites are. Are there any American Studies courses taught at Georgetown?

Andrea Tortora

Andrea Tortaro wasn't buying all the coffee-breath and the bull----
in the air. The AG was invited to campus by a center devoted to
the Constitution, yet students and faculty were told by university
officials to limit their protest to a designated "free speech zone" -- a
practice Sessions actually spoke out against during his remarks.

Nobody who reads this book is an advocate of a free speech zone.
Next step is for wives and husbands to begin to section off their
homes so that only the right speech is conducted in the right
section of the residence. Let's not get into anything specific here
right now.

Tortaro said: "For me, the idea of zoning free speech is personal.
When my alma mater of Ohio University, a public institution,
recently unveiled what it calls a "Freedom of Expression" policy, I
did a double take. Did I mention my major? Journalism. That's
right, I learned about the First Amendment at the very institution
that now is trying to quash free expression...In name, OU's
interim policy is Orwellian. As it stands, the code severely restricts
freedom of expression by effectively banning free speech within
any campus building."

"It states: Demonstrations, rallies, public speech-making,
picketing, sit-ins, marches, protests, and similar assemblies are not
permitted in the interior spaces of university buildings. This
provision shall not limit the right of groups or individuals to
reserve available facilities."

" The policy also allows the university to designate outdoor free speech zones as it sees fit. It's alarming how common this tactic of zoning free speech -- like it's a building code -- is becoming on our college campuses.

"The Foundation for Individual Rights in Education concludes that about 1 in 10 colleges and universities have zoned free speech."

"By making parts of a public university campus off limits for free speech, Ohio University and other schools restrict people -- especially students and faculty -- from exercising their rights to freedom of expression."

"I would be a completely different person today if the current policy had been in place when I was a student. I spent most of my time at Baker Center, where students, faculty and other groups used to congregate for demonstrations, because the student newspaper office is housed there."

Thank you, Andrea.

Chapter 5 Should I Run for the House, or the US Senate?

Are Catholic Colleges immune from the direction of Bishops?

A short while ago, we were discussing a Scranton PA University, namely, Marywood, where I was once employed. I am still fond of Marywood in many ways. I am also fond of Notre Dame, because of their football legacy for sure. However, like many conservatives and Catholics, I was not too fond of ND when they gave an anti-Catholic president an honorary degree and respectfully permitted his speech at graduation ceremonies in 2009.

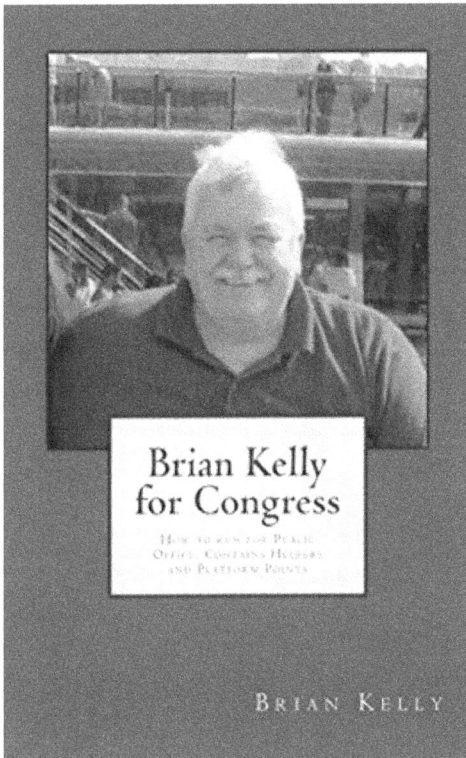

Brian Kelly
for Congress

How to win the Public
Office. Contains Helpers
and Platform Points

BRIAN KELLY

I don't think Bishop Martino would have given the ND extravaganza with somebody who was not a friend of Catholicism, a green light.

Marywood was very kind to candidate Obama in 2008 when Obama signs and placards were everywhere on campus and the whole campus was an Obama free-speech zone. I noticed as did many conservatives including Fred Flagel, as noted previously that the opposition had no voice on campus. Marywood had become an instrument of the Democratic Party, or so it seemed. Marywood and Notre Dame were both very kind to non-Catholics with political opinions mirroring those of progressives and opposed to Christians.

As a Catholic and as a Christian--non-redundant terms, while he was in office, I feared that Barack H. Obama was not the great uniter, as he claimed to be. Once he was elected I did hope that as an African American, he would help end the residue of strife that was left between blacks and whites. Instead, he had a chip on his shoulder and he made the situation worse. He created the new racism in America. Before Obama, I cannot recall the issue being played so often.

Obama became our president because many whites felt that he had solved the problem of black and white in America, and that he would make it all right. Many of us prayed that we were right. But, instead, he made it all worse. Though he was reared in a mostly white family and professed love for his white mother and grandparents, he could not control his own anti-white bias.

Whether we wanted him to win or not, few feared an Obama Administration that would bridge the color difference and make us all Americans.

Unfortunately, the theoretically non-political Obama, and the non-racist Obama failed to show up at all for a meeting in his eight years as president. All we got was politics and racism, racism, racism. What a blown opportunity for the black community. What a blown opportunity for a smart black president. I did not vote for him for other than race reasons. Our ideologies do not even intersect.

However, I was hoping he would preside well as I would have done what I could do to make sure he solved the ills of our country—if that was what he really wanted. As it turns out, it was not what he wanted or both blacks and whites would have seen some progress in that regard. Obama was a divider; not a uniter. He enjoyed highlighting differences and not similarities, and if he had any love for America, he kept it well-masked.

About ten years before I was promoted to Assistant Professor at Marywood University, I had taken a great retirement package from the IBM Corporation. My first six post-IBM years were at College Misericordia, teaching part time in Computer Science and Business Information Technology, while holding a full-time job as the chief technology officer for the institution.

Marywood had been my account as a Senior IBM Systems Engineer at IBM and so I was well known on campus even after I retired from IBM. I served as a consultant and a graduate faculty professor at the time Marywood sought me out to join the faculty half-time while a good friend took the other half of the Business Information Technology position.

My great lifetime friend Dennis Grimes, who had taught at Marywood for many years, while I had been supporting the institution on the technical side as an IBM employee and later as a technology consultant, accepted a shared faculty position with me. It was a pro-rata position for each of us meaning that instead of being paid by the course, we each got a pro-rata share of a full-time professor salary. In other words, we got a half-salary each as well as certain benefits that were not available to part-timers.

When the candidate Obama was running for his first term, Marywood's mostly liberal faculty and administration, from top to bottom were very excited. I do not know the source of the faculty support or administrative support but as already discussed, Obama signs were everywhere you could go on campus. Advocates were allowed to do anything for Obama.

His Republican opponent, John McCain had no voice. His image and his platform were absent from this large NEPA campus. Fred Fagel, the loyal opposition at the time, was not even a voice crying out in the desert. Republicans were hiding under rocks as they knew they were targets if they were against the anointed one.

It was easy to notice that Marywood had made its choice as an institution. As a Catholic and as a Christian, I questioned this to myself, but I had just been hired and I left it to others to fight the Catholic battle on campus at this time if they chose to do so. The force for Obama was so deep, nobody offered a countervailing thought. It would not have been well received.

I was a fairly popular national tech book author in the 1990's through 2010. Many of my books were adopted by colleges teaching IBM AS/400 courses. Ironically, after a refreshing that I gave a number of my tech books just over a year ago, these books have begun to sell quite well. Marywood had adopted several of my tech books during this time period.

I do not recall the exact number of the tech books that I had written by 2010, and let me assure you, you would not want to know their titles, but the Business Department faculty was very pleased with my "excessive" publishing. They highlighted my tech books in a trophy case in The Business Hall.

To me, it was a great honor. It seemed to be mutual as I was a national author on the very technology that Marywood was deploying to both run the business of the institution and to teach students.

Working half time at the institution gave me lots of time to write. As noted, I had been hired as an instructor on the faculty for a shared position, but in 2007, I was promoted to Assistant Professor. My evaluations were always well above par. Even millennials, who I often had to discipline for cheating or for other negative behavior, chose not to hammer me on evals.

My evals kept getting better and better and so the University bypassed its normal procedures and promoted me early and from a pro-rata position, which was especially unusual. I became an Assistant Professor by rank and that itself was unusual in an era in which PhD's, whether they could teach or not; whether they could speak English or not; were preferred in the classroom over M.B.A.'s.

I was well aware that in Academia, your livelihood depended on the Administration finding your student evaluations favorable to students. I had never worked for high student evaluations, just individual competency but I did well enough to warrant a promotion. When I left the institution, my official rank was Assistant Professor.

To the best of my knowledge, it did not matter at all if your students could even spell computer as long as they thought you were a great guy and they said so in their all-important evaluations.

Was I fired for running for office?

Never giving a thought to the political ramifications at Marywood, and the possibility of being fired for running for office, I put my hat in the ring for the US Congress in 2010. I was making a living with my IT consultancy, and being a tech book author, I was selling lots of tech books and making real dollars at the time. So, although I valued my university position, I decided it was my time to jump in and do one for the big Gipper—meaning the USA. I decided to run for Congress from my home district in Pennsylvania.

Obama was just elected President, and I was not very pleased with the division that he was already causing the country. The Northeastern PA Democratic Party was endorsing the same thirteen-term incumbent named Paul Kanjorski, who, most in my home town felt had been in office long enough. Without giving you a blow-by blow, I took no contributions, bought some T-shirts, and some yard signs, and gave it a shot. I did it like you would do it if you had not grown up in politics.

A great bunch of non-political friends and I got fifteen hundred signatures to make it to the Congressional ballot. One thousand were needed. In the state lottery for ballot position, 100 miles away, the Capitol Police pulled my name up to be #1 candidate on the PA Primary Ballot in 2010.

No official from my school, Marywood, who loved the grants the prior Congressman had brought to them regularly, nor my local party chiefs, were interested in switching horses to my candidacy, when they had a 13-term, 26-year Democrat shoe-in on the ballot.

And, so, though a Democrat myself of the unrecognized conservative variety, I was not even contacted by the establishment. I was treated as the not-so-loyal opposition. I had to be defeated by the Democratic Party. They did not control me. The people however, even Democrats, were not for the Party in this race. They wanted the incumbent to be defeated.

I was advised by friends at Marywood not to do anything that would assure that the University knew what I was doing politically. They suggested that if I were planning to post signs or anything, I had better get official permission.

When I requested the same accommodations that the university had given candidate Obama, who was not a member of the Marywood faculty at the time. the administration was anything but cordial.

When I requested such permission; they told me flat out "no." There were still leftover Obama signs on campus to prove that their response to me me was ad-hoc and not a real policy. They fired Fred Fagel over his protestations about his signs being ripped down on campus. To this day, I do not really know how they were legally able to fire me, but that is not the purpose of this book. I think that Marywood's campus ought to be declared a political zone. "Trust this administration at your own risk."

I found it ironic that they would support Obama but not one of their own for national office. In the "piling on category", they also told me that I could not carry my nomination petition on campus. Moreover, Marywood officials told me point blank that if any of my campus friends, i.e. faculty peers who wanted to sign my petition, it was *verboten* to do so on campus.

Any Brian W. Kelly signings had to be done off campus. They never cited faculty manual paragraphs, but they were very determined to keep me from winning,

Though they could not cite the paragraphs in the faculty handbook, the officials at Marywood directed me that I could not use the name Marywood in any of my campaigning. That was tougher to do than anything else as I was not sure how to tell the press that I could not reveal my employer's name, but I was not unemployed.

How good would it have been for me to tell those making inquiries that my company was not rooting for me and had said that I could not mention their name during the campaign. I knew that I had to say that I worked for Marywood University, so I did exactly that. The more I said that, I must admit the sorrier I felt for Marywood University that they would put me through that for the sake of their socialist / progressive agenda.

I had not been fired yet. Somebody in the administration must have discovered my mentioning that I worked at Marywood, so I had to be fired. However, the more constraints Marywood placed on me, the more I wished I had never met this university.

How did this all happen?

A multi-term commissioner in Lackawanna County, where Marywood is located, also entered the Primary. He had visited me on campus with apparent permission and told me that his pollsters reported that I would get no more than 4% of the vote. He did his best to talk me into getting off the ballot, so he could beat the incumbent.

I was not ready to trust anybody except the good people who had worked to get me on the ballot. So, I did not heed the pleas of the Commissioner. I suspect that there would have been other gratuities and favors that would have come my way if I agreed and he had won. I wanted none of what he was selling.

The incumbent won and the other challenger, the Commissioner, who was well known in the adjacent county got about twice the # of votes as me. I picked up 17% and was proud of my accomplishment. I had learned how dirty politics really is. Together, our vote count beat the incumbent. Even with less than 50%, the incumbent still got the nomination.

The pundits in NEPA could not believe that I had gotten 17% of the votes in our district in my first political attempt without really spending campaign level cash. I knew that it was from the groundswell of people that wanted major change, which I had promised. Why else would I have run?

I was upset that the incumbent won the Democratic Primary, but I had done my best. I contacted the Republican Challenger Lou Barletta and I asked if I could help him. People are far more important than Party.

Mr. Barletta asked me to become the Democrat liaison to his campaign and I agreed to do so. I gave some speeches and was available for any work needed. I built a web site for Democrats to learn more about the candidate. Congressman Barletta won the race. He is now running for the US Senate. He is a good man.

I am still happy about what I did to help even though it cost me my job at Marywood. I continue to have a good relationship with the Congressman, who hopefully soon will be the Junior Senator from Pennsylvania.

I know the precepts of the Catholic Church from eight years at St. Boniface Grade School; years as an altar boy; and years as a lector at Mass. The precepts do not include nasty retribution against political opponents. Perhaps Marywood did not get the same lessons as I.

Nonetheless, within a week or so of Barletta becoming our new Congressman, Marywood, a Catholic Institution that was embarrassed that I gave the sitting Congressman, their benefactor, a tough go in the Primary and then supported his opponent in the fall, told me that it was my last contract.

I had just recently been promoted from Instructor to Assistant Professor. For Marywood, this was a major accomplishment. I had already broken tradition gaining a faculty position after having been an adjunct for several years. Adjuncts are typically not promoted to regular faculty.
Marywood University made up an excuse that was a bold-face lie after they fired me because I had run for public office. It should not have mattered what side I was on. I learned that even Catholic Universities are not beyond politics. My Chairman brought me in to his office a week after the election and gave me the bad news.

Politics is a dirty business even when administered by an academic instrument of the Catholic Church. Having lied to me, I well understood why the institution would not take on the coffee-breath liberal arts professors who were lying through their teeth to convince millennials that being a US citizen was no big deal in a world in which the US was the big problem.

Chapter 6 Are Millennials the Dumbest Generation?

Do Millennials Stand a
Chance in the Real World?

The Worst Generation?

Nothing Will Solve McDonald's
Millennial Problem

AND I GUESS SOMEONE IS BUYING THESE BOOKS?

THE
DUMBEST
GENERATION

NOT
EVERYONE
GETS A
TROPHY

BRUCE TULGAN

BRAVE, BRAVE, INVESTIGATIVE JOURNALISM HERE. WERE THESE PEOPLE
NEVER YOUNG ONCE? (OR THEY WERE AND THAT'S THE PROBLEM.) THE
SUPPOSED PROBLEMS WITH MILLENNIALS ARE THINGS PEOPLE HAVE BEEN
WORRYING ABOUT SINCE FOREVER.

How can smart people be so dumb?

The older you are in America today, the more confused you must
be about our youngest Americans. It is a conundrum. Can it be
that the most educated generation in American history is also the
most confused about life, politics and, especially, simple
economics. The only conclusion that can be reached from the data
is that young Americans enjoy being dumb and they will resist

being smarter, the harder anybody tries to help them. And, so, of course, they find their coffee-breath professors as bastions of good feelings while spewing lies instead of the truth.

It is to some in Academia a challenging, irksome fact that we live in what the Oxford English Dictionary calls a post-truth culture. Millennials are the pawns that are used as the tools of those thick in the culture.

Too many people, especially in politics, government, and academia tend to make up lies when it suits their emotional needs all the time, regardless of generational differences. However, a corollary in the post-truth culture is as one colleague has written "that millennials seem to lie, at least at their colleges, as if the fabric of the universe were simply malleable to pleasing their own wishes. I have seen even those students who seem most bright and most wholesome make bald faced lies to their classmates and to me; they just do it as if it came naturally and they don't seem to have any conscience about it."

Post-Truth America

It is actually tough to be a good person in such a world. Rod Dreher, writing in The American Conservative in November 17, 2016, hits the nail on the head about the problem with millennials and the truth in a piece titled: "A Professor In Post-Truth America".

"Not long ago, one student spoke to me in casual conversation of telling her club on campus an absolutely outrageous lie (I forget what it was precisely, but it was on the scale of "I survived cancer" or "I was raised in Germany). She mentioned it because she could see at some point she was going to have to pay the piper, but her disbelief went beyond that. She herself was stunned that she could just make things up out of thin air and pass them off as truth to people with whom she was going to spend hours a week for several years in a block. It wasn't so much shame, so far as I could tell, as an incomprehension at this odd and troubling power that just happened to be right there inside her.

" Here's a more irksome one: several years ago, a student lied to me about something and then, out of necessity, confessed he had lied to me. He had requested an official document from me and had lied about why he wanted it for no apparent reason as it was the kind of document I would routinely provide to him as part of my duties as a professor. I had initially just given him some information and not said document, because the lie he told did not indicate he would really need it.

"When he confessed his lying and asked again, I was insulted by his dishonesty and ignored his request. Out of desperation, he wrote again, saying something like "I'm sorry [as in, it sounds as if he is apologizing for lying] but I didn't think I would be in this bad position [as in, caught lying and with no alternative but to confess]." He actually said he was truly sorry not because he had been dishonest (again, for no apparent reason), but because he had been put in the horrible position of having to confess to a lie. "Sorry for being caught" doesn't quite capture the absurdity of his statement.

"Has this happened in your workplace? Asking seriously. I have a Millennial friend who changed the focus of her studies at one of the nation's top medical schools after she observed rampant, conscious fraud among her student colleagues in the research lab. I asked her if she was talking about things as egregious as falsifying data. Absolutely, she said. The reason was competition for status and research grants. They just did not care. She did not want to be co-opted by that system.

"She was not talking about lawyers, or liberal arts professors, or anybody like that. She was talking about research scientists.

"It's not quite the same thing as this, but closely related: Dante believed that the loss of belief in the sacred and binding qualities of vows was behind the social and civic collapse of

Italy in the High Middle Ages. He discerned that if people believed that their word was only valid when they believed it advanced their interests, things would inevitably fall apart. This is why Traitors were in the lowest pit of Hell: because when you cannot trust the word of anybody, not even your neighbor, a stable society becomes impossible."

A privileged generation?

From the day they were born, today's young Americans above 20 years of age, have received more attention than any generation in the history of man. They are convinced the world revolves around them and their many participation trophies, and the liberal mindsets and the coffee-breath professors on college campuses are the perfect reinforcement to their beliefs. They believe their professors are substitute nannies and of course, their hard left-leaning nannies would never lead them astray. That's just how it is.

Of course, there are other reasons to blame for the dumbness and for the liberal bias they hold. First, they're just plain young, and young people are typically to the left of the rest of the country on social and economic issues. Second, they are the most diverse adult demographic in American history, and minorities have historically been to the left of the country as well. Third, even young white men and women are more liberal than their parents, particularly on three social issues—gay rights, immigration, and marijuana—and generally on their willingness to accept more government involvement in income redistribution and universal health care. Their overwhelming support for Obama was the most any young group has leaned toward a Democrat since 1972.

Many are angry about their education and their huge student debt. They have nothing, and their future is not bright. Education once promised a full social contract as a degree always produced a job, and the job procured a good middle-class life or better. Now the debt of school and the flood of immigrants into US jobs has created a perfect storm: Low youth wages that make it hard to pay off record-high student debt. Maybe millennials have a beef but becoming a liberal socialist to solve their problem is like checking into debtor's prison to pay off student loans. Neither will work.

It is time for a little bit of humor to make a point. Millennials clearly know who they are and don't seem to care who we are. Thus, they may not know the impact they have on the rest of us.

I recently found an email from a good friend, an octogenarian. I just read it. It describes well the impact of liberal millennials on the rest of us. Enjoy!

What am I ??

I used to think I was just a normal person.,

But.....I was born white, which now, whether I like it or not, makes me a racist.

I am a fiscal and moral conservative, which by today's standards, makes me a fascist.

I am heterosexual, which according to gay folks, now makes me a homophobe.

I am a Christian, which now labels me as an infidel.

I am retired, which makes me useless.

I think, and I reason; therefore, I doubt much that the main stream media tells me, which must make me a reactionary.

I am proud of my heritage and our inclusive American culture, which makes me a xenophobe.

I value my safety and that of my family and I appreciate the police and the legal system, which makes me a right-wing extremist.

I believe in hard work, fair play, and fair compensation, according to each individual's merits, which today makes me an anti-socialist.

I believe in the defense and protection of the homeland for and by all citizens, which now makes me a militant.

Funny…it's all just taken place over the last 8 years! [written in early 2017]

As if all this B.S. wasn't enough to deal with, now that I need to use it more every day, I'm not sure which public restroom to use.

Thank you for indulging me.

There have been a number of punishments from an old bird's perspective that came with all of this. The financial punishment of the last eight years (Obama years), for example, has inspired several protest movements that have captured young liberals' imagination. Occupy Wall Street might not have produced a clear policy prescription, but it told a simple, true, and easy to understand story: The recovery had been extraordinary for the stock market and disappointing for the labor market.

When you search "profit high wages low," your search engine will dutifully bring back about 100 million results. The first pages will tell you the same story: Corporate profits reached a modern high at the same time that labor's share of national American income reached a modern low.

How many Occupy protesters, minimum-wage advocates, and Bernie Sanders supporters know that fact? It's tough to say. How many feel it? Probably 100 percent. With student loan debt and the default rate at an all-time high, and jobs and wages at all-time lows, there are ample happenings out there to wipe a smile off an otherwise charming young American.

It is not hard to know

Millennial politics is simple, really. There are few mysteries. They enjoyed their four to eight years of undergraduate education more than most generations and so, especially those who have not made their first student-loan payment, young people support big government, unless it costs them more money. They're for smaller government, unless budget cuts scratch a program they've heard about. They'd like Washington to fix everything, just as long as it doesn't run anything. That's all from a new Reason Foundation poll, surveying 2,000 young adults between the ages of 18 and 29.

To *net it out* as my friends in IBM always said, we know at least these three things about millennials:

1. Millennials are more liberal than the rest of the country, particularly on social issues, but they get more economically conservative when they make more money.
2. Millennials don't know what they're talking about when it comes to economics.
3. Far less important, but entertaining nonetheless: Millennials don't know what socialism is, but they think it sounds nice Forty-two percent of Millennials think socialism is preferable to capitalism, but only 16 percent of Millennials can accurately define socialism.
4. If their coffee-breath professors are for it—I mean anything--so are they.

Are Young Americans Dumb?

In an article from about two-years ago, Oct 25, 2016, titled, **YOUNG AMERICANS ARE DUMB**, Walter E. Williams shared a lot of statistics that show a high dolt factor among college-age people.

http://www.wnd.com/2016/10/young-americans-are-dumb/

I would love the opportunity to hear Walter E. Williams speak at one of our ten college campuses here in Northeastern, PA. Williams is almost as revered in philosophical and political circles as E.F. Hutton is in the financial world. When Walter E. Williams speaks, people listen .

Last year, Williams could not contain himself about young Americans anymore and so he wrote a great column for World Net Daily titled: Young Americans Are Dumb.

I am afraid that he is right. You may be also as you are reading this book.

It should not be quite so self-evident that younger Americans, aka millennials, typically between ages of 18 and 36 are dumb. But, it is. Especially if you are not in that age group. Williams gets our juices flowing on the topic immediately in his opening paragraph. He has a way with words.

"Prior to capitalism, the way people amassed great wealth was by looting, plundering and enslaving their fellow man. Capitalism made it possible to become wealthy by serving your fellow man."

Walter E. Williams

"Do you wonder why Sen. Bernie Sanders and his ideas are so popular among American college students? The answer is that they, like so many other young people who think they know it all, are really uninformed and ignorant. You say, "Williams, how dare you say that?! We've mortgaged our home to send our children to college."

Williams then continues his piece with a recitation of the facts to prove his thesis. He cites the 2006 geographic literacy survey of youngsters between 18 and 24 years of age by National Geographic and Roper Public Affairs.

Surprise, Surprise! Actually, for those living today and watching what gives on college campuses, there is no surprise at all.

Not even half of the respondents in the literacy survey could identify New York and Ohio on a map of the US. It was not a world map. It was just the US. Sixty percent could not find Iraq or Saudi Arabia on a map of just the Middle East. They are huge countries. Three quarters could not find Iran or Israel.

As hard as it is to believe, 44 percent could not locate even one of those four countries. The survey results mirrored the "men on the street" dummies who are often interviewed in New York City by TV personalities. Young Americans who had once taken a geography class did not do much better.

Walter E. Williams gave his age away by relating that he attended elementary school during the 1940s. Like many of us who attended grammar school in the forties, fifties, and sixties, Williams experienced the geography tests with the blank U.S. maps. The work assignment was to write in the states. Williams notes that: "Today such an assignment might be deemed oppressive, if not racist."

Williams continued: "According to a Philadelphia magazine article, the percentage of college grads who can read and interpret a food label has fallen from 40 to 30. They are six times likelier to know who won "American Idol" than they are to know the name of the speaker of the House. A high-school teacher in California handed out an assignment that required students to use a ruler. Not a single student knew how."

"An article on News Forum for Lawyers titled "Study Finds College Students Remarkably Incompetent," cites a study done by the American Institutes for Research that revealed that over 75 percent of two-year college students and 50 percent of four-year college students were incapable of completing everyday tasks."

"About 20 percent of four-year college students demonstrated only basic mathematical ability, while a steeper 30 percent of two-year college students could not progress past elementary arithmetic. NBC News reported that Fortune 500 companies spend about $3 billion annually to train employees in 'basic English.'"

To me, the dumbest thing that young Americans have done to prove they are dumb is to vote for the same party that created the past eight years of economic misery for them. They won't admit that their party encourages illegal foreign nationals, through generous visa programs to attend US universities and take American jobs right when today's American millennials are ready (if ever) to enter the workforce.

Ironically, they blame the head of the government for the last eight years before Trump, for nothing. Instead, they believe their coffee-breath professors who told them it is the nasty conservatives messing things up. Of course, these gullible dummies believe them.

I am not kidding. Just about half of the eligible voters between the ages of 18 and 29 (aka, "millennials), although millennials also include people in their early-to-mid-30s) cast ballots in the past major election. The other half were too busy being dumb and telling people what they know in short sound bursts. That voting rate falls well below the estimated general voter turnout rate of roughly 58 percent.

About 55 percent of those millennials who were able to get out of bed to vote, supported Clinton. Bring on the DUMB roll. That is compared to the 60 percent who supported Obama in 2012, according to CIRCLE's analysis.

Conversely, youth support from Republicans remained relatively constant: Trump got about 37 percent of the young American vote, roughly equivalent to what Mitt Romney received in 2012. At least everybody is not stone dumb.

Just when you thought it could not get worse for millennials on the knowledge power quotient, Just Facts in 2009, reported that the Pentagon estimated that 65 percent of 17- to 24-year-olds in the U.S. were unqualified for military service because of weak educational skills, poor physical fitness, illegal drug usage, medical conditions or criminal records.

Based on the effect of a college education on these young Americans, I was surprised that one of the maladies detected by the Pentagon was not "under the influence of a liberal socialist coffee-breath professor."

In January 2014, the commander of the U.S. Army Recruiting Command estimated this figure at 77.5 percent, and in June 2014, the Department of Defense estimated this figure at 71 percent. Unlike the norm, in which people get smarter over time, it seems that millennials are enjoying bucking that trend.

Walter E. Williams wrote an earlier column in which he openly discussed the dishonesty of college officials. In his latest report, he presents even more evidence. As dumb as they are, to university officials, young Americans, unprepared for college, make up a huge income stream for universities. They are coddled and babied and they win when they take on the faculty, which is rare.

"Among high-school students who graduated in 2014 and took the ACT college readiness exam, here's how various racial/ethnic groups fared when it came to meeting the ACT's college readiness benchmarks in at least three of the four subjects: Asians, 57 percent; whites, 49 percent; Hispanics, 23 percent; and blacks, 11 percent. However, the college rates of enrollment of these groups were: Asians, 80 percent; whites, 69 percent; Hispanics, 60 percent; and blacks, 57 percent.

Something is rotten in the state of Denmark

"What I am labeling as dishonest, fraudulent or deceitful comes from the fact that many more students are admitted to college than are in fact college-ready. Admitting such students may satisfy the wants and financial interests of the higher education establishment, but whether it serves the interests of students, families, taxpayers and the nation is another question."

Trying to begin counting at #4 for example, fails to recognize the importance of other numbers such as #1, #2, or #3.

Because every Freshman class arrives dumber than the last, colleges have adapted to the quality problem by watering down the requirements with lower standards. They have also abandoned traditional evaluation tools and topics and the focus now almost entirely is on pleasing the students. And the students know it. Ask any faculty member the source of the major measurement for their performance as a teacher. No contest—the student evaluations. Faculty live or die by student evaluations. It is more important than speaking English. I know.

In the three to five minutes it may take to read about ten of these paragraphs, a typical reader will have put in almost exactly the time that an average 15- to 24-year-old now spends reading from all sources each day. Our youngest generations have no time for the mundane aspects of life such as reading.

For example, when they encounter big gobs of text on the Internet, they find them daunting--maybe even boring. Hey! Who has the time? Besides, reading such stuff might cause you to miss a friend's Facebook status update!

Mark Bauerlein has a deep fear for our country. He is a 49-year-old professor of English at Emory University. His book, "The Dumbest Generation," tells it all. Walter E. Williams is not alone in his observations.

Like Williams, Bauerlein sees something new and disastrous that has happened to America's youth. The arrival of the instant gratification go-go-go digital age has helped nobody. Instead, it ushered in a "collective loss of context and history, a neglect of enduring ideas and conflicts"

Williams and Bauerlein cite surveys—one after the other—that painstakingly recount what most already suspect: "America's youth know virtually nothing about history and politics. And no wonder. They have developed a brazen disregard of books and reading." They actually seem to know little about little.

Bauerlein, a former Director of Research and Analysis at the National Endowment for the Arts, notes that it was not supposed to be this way. After all, "never have the opportunities for education, learning, political action, and cultural activity been greater. But somehow, the much-ballyhooed advances of this brave new world have not only failed to materialize -- they've actually made us dumber." Of course, it begins with the young, but it doesn't end when this batch of young Americans get older.

What is the solution?

Like many things in life, there are many solutions. Students mortgaging their lives to become indentured servants to loan sharks and College Financial Aid Counsellors no longer seems to be the best way. In fact, there is lots of evidence to suggest why the best and brightest students of America's high schools should simply consider skipping college. Why risk their intelligence to the dumbed-down teachers who have gone off to smell and drink the fine coffee in the faculty lounge.

The college campuses of the country have been taken over by angry, entitlement-driven, snowflake-minded, uneducated, untrained, undisciplined masses, who use their places of higher learning not so much to learn, but rather to advance their little propaganda campaigns. And of course, they are assisted all too frequently by socialist-minded coffee-breath professors who pine for their time as 1960s-era activist youths, when the coffee and the smoke were much stronger.

They seek causes to champion, rather than an education to gain. They love being part of every black, illegal immigrant, female, minority and LGBTQ etc. cause that comes along. It is their calling. They renounce their own whiteness. One need only peruse a few school-related headlines to see the demise of our college campuses, the political activism of our college professors, the whiny behaviors of lazy student bodies, and the major intolerance to freedom of thought, and of course that damned "other thought.".

"Professors pledge to 'decolonize curricula' to fight 'privilege,' " blasted one headline from Campus Reform, in a story about American University professors concerned about the fate of black female students forced to deal with the "stresses of living amid white supremacy."

Another, from mid-May from The Blaze: "Liberal college snowflake has epic screaming meltdown after she sees pro-Trump sign on campus."

Though we septuagenarians may find it amusing at times, the millennials are as they are because we failed to bring them up properly. It is their fault for sure, but it is also ours. After not teaching them well, we destroyed their opportunities by bringing in competing students (illegal foreign nationals) who, when they graduate will work for starvation wages. We let our politicians forget about Americans and we reward them with reelection.

Chapter 7 Should Millennials Be Forgiven?

The Pope, as Christ's Vicar on Earth is forgiving

The government is not your friend

Millennials are so annoying to Generation X that the Gen Xers, trained by WC Fields to never give a sucker an even break show little pity to the millennials even when their own kids are part of the mix.

For a good record of what we are talking about, we know that different agencies use different years for generational definitions. For example, the Harvard Center uses a birth from 1965 to 1984 to define Gen X so that Boomers, Xers, and Millennials "cover equal 20-year age spans". They conclude that immigration filled in any birth year deficits during low fertility years of the late 1960s and early 1970s. Immigration, legal and illegal has never been a friend of millennials whether they know it or not.

Despite self-serving governmental, political, and academic apologists suggesting that there is no real student debt crisis, just ask a recent millennial graduate when they hope to start a family. You better have a lot of time. We keep hearing about a student debt crisis. Yet, politicians continue to argue that there is no student debt crisis though everybody else knows that there is. Perhaps the definition of a crisis can tell us--*a time of intense difficulty, trouble, or danger.*

The fact is that recent students with major loans are having trouble paying them back. The fact is that they have put off major life plans until their personal crisis improves to manageable.

Is the country in crisis? Whether the country is in crisis or not, taxpayers are now on the hook for about $1.45 trillion outstanding in student debt but as of now at least, most of that is being paid back. That total does make student debt substantially larger even than credit card debt, however. I mean all credit card debt. Moreover, it's not looking like it's going to get any better in the future. The graduating class of 2018 owed an average of over $39,000, up from less than $30,000 in 2014.

In this regard, it is OK for all Americans to have some pity on millennials as they did not ask to be in the veritable debtor's prison in which they have been placed by our government.

The real problem is many problems

The people that say there is not a student debt crisis suggest that most people will repay their debts though it may take them 10 to 20 years to do it. The real problem, these people believe, is the expanding default rate on student loans. Just a couple years ago, the defaulters were at 7 million. Now 8 million former students no longer pay a dime back.

Your friendly US Department of Education produced a report recently that noted the two-year cohort default rate on student loans increased from 9.1% for FY 2010 to 10% for FY 2011 In 2017, the default rate has already climbed to 11.2% and the average monthly out of pocket student loan payment for a borrower aged 20 to 30 years is $351. That is a good part of a mortgage payment or a full payment on a family car.

It cannot be argued that more student debtors are falling behind on their federal student loans. The share of Americans at least 31 days late on loans from the U.S. Department of Education ticked up to 18.8 percent as of June 30, 2-17, up from 18.6 percent the same time the prior year.

As noted, the total in US student loan debt has climbed to $1.45 trillion and as of right now, about 45 million Americans have some student loan debt.

Most experts say the program is operating in crisis mode.

Who's to blame?

The easiest people to blame for these problems are, of course, the students. After all they are the ones who took out the loans. However, like your dad and my dad would say, "What do they know?" That's actually the problem.

For some reason, which I admit has little merit, we here in the US have decided that the norm for every child born in America is to have a college education. Consequently, I would suspect we have the worst electricians, plumbers, and auto mechanics in the world as we have basically shut down the vocational technical training once a mainstay in high school.

From what I have observed, the richest guys in many towns today run the plumbing businesses, electrical businesses, and of course body shops and vehicle repair shops. My cousin Frank, who is a great guy by the way, made his millions in New Jersey by being the one body shop in his home town. Now, he makes a few bucks in a different way. He bought about 300 acres in a PA town that is producing fracking gas in a big way.

Guys like cousin Frank are tickled that many of their future competitors opt to get college degrees. It follows that when they have to pay off the loans for those degrees, they will not have the cash to build a new garage in town to compete against cousin Frank. That may help guys like Frank in that business, but it does not help America overall.

The supposed plusses of having to have a degree, for years has convinced the vast majority of US high schools to dedicate their efforts to getting their students prepared for a college education. With so many in America possessing four-year degrees today, the sheepskin is often worth little more than the cost of the ink and the parchment. I suspect that the sheep would balk at giving up their skin for such an iffy arrangement.

Think about the gal or guy who sat next to you in a number of high school classes. Were they college material? When everybody, regardless of smarts became college material, colleges figured out how to bolster their income by admitting them on probations that could and would continue for four years. Students are the source of revenue for universities. Let's not forget that.

So, there are many students who put in their four years without being fully admitted and are then get kicked out without a degree, when it is obvious that they had taken enough courses to prove that they never should have been admitted in the first place. Now, these poor souls cannot find enough money to start a landscaping business, so they get a job flipping hamburgers trying to come up with $350 a month to pay off their four-year student loan. Is that a crisis? It sure is.

Somebody in a university and some coffee-breath faculty student advisor who knows colleges are in it for the money, helped convince Johnny or Janie that they could make it whether they should have a degree or not. Consequently, forty-six percent of those that start college drop out before graduating. As hard as it is to believe, one of the major reasons for this is undoubtedly the fact that many should never have been admitted to any self-respecting college in the first place.

But, we may forget sometimes that colleges are a business also and businesses must survive by having customers who can pay their bills. How wonderful for these institutions with no hearts, that Johnny and Janie equally were able to get a guaranteed student loan so that College A could be assured of receiving their full tuition even if neither student had a chance for success.

Another part of the problem is that most seventeen and eighteen-year old's have mush brains and they use valedictorians as models when they are trying to eke out a C in Gym class. Yes, all valedictorians will graduate from college unless they rig the game against themselves. But, most high school students sporting a C average ought to try to find a job as a beautician if they have dexterity, or a barber, or an auto mechanic. If they can get into plumbing or become electrical apprentices, their lives are set.

In Northeastern PA, if the McDonalds and Burger King guys get their $15.00 hourly wage, then the fully degreed sociology majors who are out working in kindness industries, will be able to up their salaries by about $10,000 and they can take over the jobs these non-degreed personnel have. Not only can these college grads flip the burgers better in most cases, they can also handle the cash register.

Additionally, management may find a great brain among them and bring them into a corporate program. So, why the degree and why the student loan for sociology or psychology if you are not headed for a PhD or an MD.

High school 17 and 18-year-old seniors, though they "know everything," are simply not prepared to choose the right college majors. But, since they have "I know everything," cards printed by their buddies in Print Shop or elsewhere to present to anybody offering counsel, it is tough to talk them out of a career in rocket science.

Sociology is the most altruistic major as the graduate gives to others all her life and she makes little more than the horse groomer at the end of town, who never spent a dime to get a degree. Nonetheless, there are other degrees similar to sociology that millennials are encouraged to pursue. For example, many choose majors that align with their passions such as film and video arts, pre-school education, psychology, anthropology, archaeology, fine arts and music. It's great work if you can get it.

Like sociology, the pursuit of knowledge in these majors might be fun and rewarding but they rarely lead to well-paying careers. For that matter, many of the young people who choose these types of careers won't even be able to find jobs. In fact, as of March 2012, 60% of college graduates were unable to find work in their fields of study. Trump is making getting a job easier and perhaps soon, the pay increases will come with the. But, right now. College graduates in the sociology area need to volunteer to help in Food Kitchens for the poor so they too can eat well.

I have seen statistics that suggest that about 80% of college graduates have no choice but to return to the roost and let mom and dad continue paying their big bills in life. No wonder the Democrats think we need illegal aliens to do the jobs in America that Americans never trained themselves to do well.

Colleges and universities are big culprits in the student loan crisis

It is an understatement to suggest that colleges and universities are at least partially to blame for the student debt problem, especially the for-profit schools. Whether they admit it or not, all colleges and universities other than the finest of the well-endowed, are in a competitive business.

Please permit me to tell you a secret that is not such a secret in the boardrooms of our country's most successful universities. It is as clear as day when you follow the prospects of students who matriculate after much consideration. They contemplate whether they should be greeting card designers or plumbers or college graduates.

While they are in such deep thought, a great number of them are enticed by local counselors with affinities to certain colleges or by various program counsellors in universities that need students to enroll to assure revenue. To get the revenue, the counsellors present loans packages that the prospective students cannot ever afford even with a degree in the art of leisure. That is the first reason why there are so many loan defaults.

Traditional 50 and 100-year old colleges and / or universities that would be classified as non-profit endowment based institutions, are more likely to tell the truth to a high-school flunky, who thinks he should go to college. The flunky wants to go to college often because the girlfriend is going to the same college. Many otherwise bad future marriages would be on the verge of collapse today if the admirer was not already rejected by the institution for lack of cranial substance.

Not all traditional non-profit colleges are so appropriate as to actually deny admittance to a poor scholar. *For-profit* colleges and universities are the worst at grubbing for money from the young chump who wants to be a college graduate because his girlfriend is smart enough to be one.

Under the covers, *For-profits'* admissions departments are run as marketing departments. Marketing to students nobody else wants is their mission. The loan amount and the loan default rates are the highest at these institutions of higher-priced learning. When they default, American taxpayers are again left holding the debt bag, even though the institution is private.

As an example, students that borrow similar amounts to pay for their schooling end up defaulting at a much higher rate at for-profit institutions. In fact, 26% of for-profit students that took out loans between $5000 in $10,000 ended up defaulting versus the 10% of students at community colleges that defaulted and the 7% at four-year traditional schools.

Private schools are not immune to this either. They, too, must compete for students. The more aid they can offer prospective students, the more they will attract. This puts pressure on them to accept "marginal" students and for their financial aid offices to promote federal student loans as a way to pay for their educations.

Yet, I have not seen any academic institution in any of the categories from traditional to for-profit ever suggest that the huge assets of the major academies and the lesser capabilities of the lesser endowed, should join together to help the poor students, who tried in their institutions but failed, to be rescued in any way.

All of their profits are their profits and they choose to use no profits to help their failed products, their graduates, get through the loan costs needed to have a little chance in life.

Maybe we should remind Academia that they are not supposed to be profit making snobs. Their mission is the education of young adults.

Chapter 8 Is the Student Loan Game Rigged?

Do Colleges and Universities have an unfair advantage?

You bet they do!

It costs Academic Institutions nothing when students come out sacked with a lifetime of debt after four to six years with no jobs. Donald Trump can recognize a rigged game better than any man in America. He can sniff them out and call them out and /or play against them and still win. He thinks the student loan game is rigged against students and it favors the universities and the government disguised as loan sharks.

Trump does not like that the game is rigged, and he has promised to fix it. The President believes that Universities must have some skin in the game for any long-term solutions to be built.

Many people are affected by the crisis and, so it is a topic at the dinner table in many homes—especially in those homes in which the student loan invoices are beginning to arrive from junior's or missy's four or five-year past sojourn into campus life.

When people in the US discuss the student debt crisis, most focus on how it affects them personally. If they are not directly affected themselves or through their extended families, they discuss the rapid growth in outstanding debt and its impact on the economy and the country.

They may also discuss some of the recent milestones, which are not very positive. For example, student loan debt exceeded credit card debt in 2010 and it exceeded auto loan debt in 2011. It is rapidly rising, and it passed the $1 trillion mark in 2012. It is currently at about $1.45 trillion and growing rapidly. Such a burgeoning debt, which must be paid back by millennials trying to make it in a tough world, is not good for America.

It is a big problem. The Wall Street Journal recently reported that More than 40% of student loan borrowers are either in default, delinquency or have postponed repaying their student loans. It is a crisis and having the federal government making over $45 billion off the backs of student borrowers in excessive interest payments does nothing to help matters.

With about 40% of students defaulting on their loan paybacks—mostly because the payments are so large, is a problem for all America. It is also a big disgrace for a country that does not want to be labeled as "Third World."

These milestones don't tell us much about the impact of all that debt on the students themselves. Seventeen and Eighteen-year-olds are making lifetime decisions in High School still today with little unbiased counselling other than "Don't Worry! Be Happy!"

These naïve high school seniors were originally told by a friendly College Financial Aid Officer that everybody borrows, and it is a privilege to be able to attend this college with the help of the university's loan package.

Does that sound familiar. If Joe's Hot Car Lot was scamming young adults at the same rate as academia, the Justice Department would shut them down. At least Joe's Hot Cars can make it around the block. What about the kids with $100,000 in debt, no degree, and no job? They never get to see the other side of the block.

Sometimes as learned by default interviews, there was never even an up-front discussion of the loan impact for when it came time to repay it. As hard as it is to believe, the loans came so easy that 53% of the students when graduating, did not even know there was a payback. And we all know what payback is! It's a b----!

70% of all college students have borrowed and many who are already enrolled still have more to borrow before they finish their degrees. Then, before they can engage in life, they must pay for their college education. It is a national travesty. No wonder millennials are disgruntled.

America and Americans had been told by Team Obama for his eight years that we are not exceptional. The way government treats the best and the brightest, who owe huge amounts of school debt, is proof that this past president and his administration were not kidding. Student loans keep all debtors in the same rut, much like a debtor's prison. Forget about marriage, babies, cars, and homes.

Meanwhile, the past president put the government in charge of huge chunks of the student loan industry. Team Obama picked up over 40 $billion a year in profits by whacking students with high government interest rates to help pay for his Obamacare.

No matter how immune you get to hearing about government $billions here and there, remember that a $billion is an extremely large amount of money. Even a $million is quite large. A $million is so big it gives more meaning to the word billion. It is 1000 million. Would you not like to have a $million right now?

Obama's government made the debt problem worse for student loan debtors by taking more interest dollars than needed to sustain the program. Uncle Sam is on track to make $66 billion in profits this year after Uncle Obama took over the student loan program six years ago. That's why Donald Trump wants to turn the program back over to private enterprise at competitive rates.

With inflation, and with burgeoning excessive tuition costs, a college degree isn't worth much anymore. Everybody has one and the ones who should not have been admitted in the first place, are jobless, in debt up to their ears and they have no college degree. Often, they are marginal students and they have two to six more courses to go when they drop out. They are on no corporate recruiters top ten list.

Some suggest, and I agree that certain college majors ought not ever be granted loans. Professionals with sociology and philosophy degrees are not in demand. Do you know anybody who is employed as a philosopher?

Today, many students opt to continue after graduation to pursue a Master's degree. The academic community has answered the call and their rationale for no job after five years of undergraduate work is to go for an advanced degree. Yes, unabashed Universities, knowing the depleted value of their undergraduate degrees suggest that students take out more loans and get a Master's Degree. This supposedly may give them a better shot at a job or a promotion--maybe.

After five years or so, experience counts the most. IBM paid for my MBA, but it did not help me one way or another in my career. However, it did give me the minimum credentials to teach as a professor in a college, of which I took advantage for over thirty years part time, adjunct, and "full-time."

I know from my own family that students with graduate degrees have substantially higher debt. Law School graduates owe about $200,000 and MD Degrees owe as much as $500,000. If most undergraduate students were getting high paying jobs as in the past, the problem would not be as severe as they would be able to pay back their loans.

Bartenders, Waiters, and Short Order Cooks have a tough time handling the new government approved repayment rates for their undergraduate debt. Ironically, a college education is one of the few things in life that's value is going down, while its price is going up.

More and more parents are advising their less than valedictorian-level children to think about a trade or a less-skilled job, before committing a zillion dollars to a debt they may not be able to pay back.

Why is student debt increasing? Government, under Democrat control with grants and support for postsecondary education has simply chosen not kept pace with increases in college costs. Democrats have sold out American-born College students to gain the favor of the coffee-breath liberal professors in the universities. In many ways professors talk students out of being productive members of society. Look what is happening at once prestigious universities across the country.

Government money, AKA Santa Claus, has been diverted to welfare programs and other schemes that give Democrats advantages in elections. The one-time party of the people has forgotten completely about Americans, who are now saddled with huge debt repayment plans while foreign students who overstay their visas are getting their jobs by accepting lower wages.

Colleges are oblivious as nothing has hurt them. They make a ton of money while students and graduates scrounge for alms. This is their renaissance period as we find them going about like their product has no issues. They keep building new theatres, art museums, athletic centers, student centers and all kinds of amenities to attract students to make their campuses more beautiful to the eye. But, their graduates, who had one heck of a good time using all those amenities for four or five years, now are stuck paying the bill without a job.

Colleges and Universities need money to build, and heat these edifices to their success. So, the increasing burden of tuition financing has shifted paying for college from the federal and state governments to families using student loans as the preferred vehicle.

Meanwhile the colleges and universities are not investing in helping produce graduates capable of getting and holding jobs, Instead, the contest to become the college with the finest amenities, has pushed tuition charges through the roof.

Since grants and gifts and scholarships simply are not there anymore thanks to the Democrats in Congress, various types of loans in the "package" have become the primary vehicle today for unaware high school students to make the jump to college.

Bankers would be fools to finance a home or an expensive car for a high school senior, who never had a loan in her or his life. Yet, colleges and universities are encouraged by loan sharks to provide $100,000 or more in loans to seventeen-year-olds or eighteen-year olds, with no questions asked. As a professor with more than thirty years' experience, I witnessed it myself.

I know that many think that forty is the new fifty and thirty is the new twenty. Well in my observations as a professor, eighteen is the new fourteen. I was seventeen when I began college, but I know my maturity level was far more advanced than the bulk of millennials I find as students in colleges today. I graduated at 21 years of age and three weeks later I was working for IBM as a systems engineer calling on IBM computer system clients.

Repayment begins soon after graduation

Ironically, when the first loan bill comes to the home address; first the parents, then the students are shocked that they owe so much money. Yet, each year, while in school, they signed for the new loans.

Worse than that, they become convinced at the wording of the invoice that they must pay it back. Somehow, until the risk of the student withdrawing from the institution is long past, nobody from the university finds it necessary to talk about the real cost of those loans.

Can an indebted student ever get back their life?

If President Obama wanted to, I believe he could have solved this problem in eight years. He could have had Team Obama analyze and fix the student debt problem rather than have it dumped on President Trump's shoulders.

In his trusted Cabinet and his trusty Czars, there were no MBA's. It was the blind leading the blinder. There was nobody who knew anything about capitalism and how it really works. These pompous Cretans looked down on capitalism and those trying to eke out a living in business. Now millennials for their blind belief in the system are saddled with almost unrecoverable debt.

The government somehow innately knew that they had all the knowledge necessary as the great elites from the SWAMP always seem to have. Nonetheless the problem remains unsolved and nobody from the prior regime is talking about a great report by an expert brought in to solve the problem. There were no experts called in to help.

Looking at the reports about this subject freely available in many sources such as the Internet, you would soon find that students who graduate with excessive debt are about 10% more likely to say that it caused delays in their major life events, such as buying a home, getting married, or having children.

They are also about 20% more likely to say that their debt influenced their employment plans, causing them to take a job outside their field, to work more than they desired, or to work more than one job. These numbers will get worse over time, but they are already unbearable to many millennials.

Perhaps not surprisingly, they are also more likely to say that their undergraduate education was not worth the financial cost. It is a truth that American families have yet to digest. What do universities say about that?

Nobody in the biased, corrupt press is interviewing university presidents on that subject. Why? Because the press is corrupt. But, you already knew that. The Press, the progressives, and the coffee-breath professors and administrators in our colleges and universities are in cahoots. Nobody in this politically correct world would dare utter a negative word about colleges and universities. After all, they are run by liberal progressive socialists who can do no wrong, yet who somehow have.

Chapter 9 Should Generation Z Go to College?

Forget Millennials: It's All About Gen Z

- Anyone born after 1995
- Described as "conscientious, hard-working and mindful of the future"
- First true digital natives

GENERATION Z

What Should Employers Know About Gen Z?

Giving back comes first.
Gen Z favors companies with corporate social responsibility that aligns with their beliefs and values which consist of bold ideas, creativity and optimism.

Gen Z is chasing the dream job.
Gen Z is pragmatic and realistic, but they also believe it is possible to achieve their "dream job" and build a career doing what they love.

Career growth counts, too.
Opportunities for professional development are most essential when attracting Gen Z talent.

yourcareerintel

It depends is the best answer.

This was never a tough question in the past. The answer was always "YES." It is a tough question to answer nowadays. Unless you are convinced that you can be at a minimum in the top 25% of your class, and you are willing to work unbelievably hard to assure your class rank, you are better off trying to get a job right now and forego college temporarily. That is just an opinion.

From the 1960s on, there never was a question even if it were asked. "Everyone needs to go to college, right? Right." If you want any sort of job today – up to and including clerking or being an executive assistant – for years you're told you need a college degree. But does it always work out? Less and less!

And, so, some people believe that the whole idea that everyone needs to go to college is nothing more than ill-founded social engineering much the same as the idea in the early 2000s that everyone should own a house. Did you ever hear of the subprime housing crisis? Of course, you did!

Where do we go from here?

How does the thinking that right or wrong you must go to college work out in reality? Most young people who but into this idea do not have enough money to pay today's super-inflated college costs. Moreover, those who graduated with debt are having a hard time in their financial life. There is always a great solution at hand. They borrow the money.

They are not credit worthy enough to buy a moped, certainly not a motorcycle, a car or a small home. But, somehow, they can secure a loan of equal or more value that without a big job after graduation, they can never pay back.

Why does any lender take on such a risk? Because government secures the loan for them even if the student has no chance in college.

This year's college students graduated owing an average of around $39,500 only to discover that due to the poor job market they have less of a chance than ever of actually getting a good job in a field commensurate with their degrees. Too bad!

The sellers of the stuff they bought, the coffee breath professors and the big shots in the administrations in academia never agree for the student borrower to take out the big eraser and wipe their signatures off the loan documents. The kids are in it forever.

If I had a say

Since seventeen-year-olds operate as the new fourteen-year-olds today as I see it, I would suggest that nobody gets a student loan until they are the new seventeen, which would be twenty-one.

Everybody once released from college with or without a degree and almost always with a huge debt package, are looking to achieve a good-life today. Too late! Unless the fourteen-year-old in you at seventeen made the right loan decisions, you are done unless a do-nothing Congress steps up and does something.

If it became a law, all decisions by students hoping for a college degree could be made with cash. No problem. Loans would be outlawed for college degrees in my world until you were twenty-one. You could use your cash at any age and enroll. It's on the cash provider.

However, for those with no cash, and no relatives providing cash as sponsors—until they were from birth to twenty-one years-of-age, there would be no loans for them to attend any college. Once they hit twenty-one, the new seventeen, they would be granted student loan privileges.

By that time, when they reach twenty-one, hopefully, these affected millennials would have engaged in several jobs and would understand better what life is all-about.

I would suggest the following to students contemplating college today as seventeen-year-olds operating as fourteen-year-olds: Go home. Don't ruin your life. Male or female, see first if you like being an artisan, a wood craftsman, a plumber, hair-dresser, or an electrician, before you bet on the cum-line on making it big by investing $25,000 or more for year one of a college career that today is very iffy.

Unless somebody is handling your tuition other than you or a loan, "Do not go to college full-time. You are the only one taking the risk that it will help you in the future. If it does not help you; you may be strangled by debt. If you do not graduate or others beat you, big time in the class-rank area, you will suffer all your life for the mistake of choosing college over a career in another field that does not require a degree and a $100,000 loan.

Worse than that at $25,000 per year, when you find out what you want to pursue in life, it will be much less easy to achieve if you have $100,000 of debt strapped to your back. Everybody will see it. That's just the way it is.

Admittedly, these suggestions fit Generation Z more than Generation Y (millennials) as millennials for the most part are off and running, or should I say off and flailing.

I would suggest taking a few college courses at a time in your spare time and in the summer. Don't take English unless that is your love. Read a lot and write a lot. Get enrolled into a course in the discipline you might choose to follow. See if you can be an engineer. See if you can be a computer technician. See if you can be a chemist. But, do it one or two courses at a time. In all cases start with one course.

Do not take easy courses that work towards your credit requirement as you may find you don't want to be an Oceanographer but instead a diver and what a shame to have all that student debt when being a diver does not cost quite so much!

Until you absolutely must, know that so many others are swamped today by student loan debt. Mostly it is unnecessary if you don't set a four-year degree plan in motion. Do not take out any student loans. Ever! Save your life so you can be free.

What does Sue think?

When a reader named Sue commented on the ABC report of Obama's initiative on their News site, she offered the best advice I have seen in a long time to assure new students that are not now swamped by student debt, to avoid ever getting into the big student borrowing hole.

Sue responded with tremendous insight into the real problem today with student loans—the 800-pound gorilla in the room that nobody wants to talk about in an honest way.

In Sue's words: "I actually don't believe that we should put a college education in everyone's hands and think that line of thinking is part of the problem with education in this country." Sue continues:

"For decades we've restructured our elementary and high school systems to become one-size-fits-all and college is quickly going that route too. But the reality is that not everyone fits the mold. Not everyone is cut out for an office job and not everyone is cut out for construction.

"In some communities, we are now seeing a return to skills training in high schools, where kids can graduate from high school with a two-year business degree from the local community college and a cosmetology license, or a mechanics license as well as their high school diploma.

"These are kids who can go right from high school into the work force with the training they need, start working (or start their own business from their parent's garage). They won't be saddled with student loans."

"The President's program [Obama era] of encouraging students to go into debt (sorry, but a student loan is a debt) to get an education is backwards – and in the end, not everyone needs a college education to move the country forward. They simply need to be trained to do what they want to do, and preferably, they should learn it in high school." [Preferably, they should not have to be on the verge of lifetime bankruptcy when they understand their choice of professions in life.]

Bring back Kuder-like aptitude tests in HS

Back when I was in high school we took the Kuder aptitude tests to see if it would say that we should be barbers or beauticians or construction workers or accountants.

Kuder® Skills Confidence Assessment Report
Holland Clusters

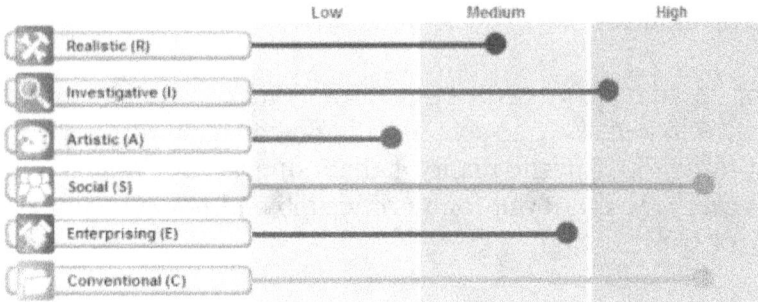

I do not know if the Kuder company is still the preferred choice but for sure a great aptitude test can help a student know whether they should attend college for a specific profession. Career aptitude tests are regularly administered in high schools throughout the country, and students anxiously await their results. Students who know what they want to be when they grow up want to see whether the results say the same.

Those with no clue what they want to be hope for some guidance. The purpose of a career aptitude test is to help provide students with an overview of their skills and begin to give them some direction for the future. The tests do not require students to choose college.

Career aptitude tests come in multiple forms. Some tests offer a series of statements about their interests and emotions. Students then indicate how well the statements relate to them. Other tests have students answer a series of multiple choice questions and use their areas of strengths and weaknesses to determine potential careers.

Tests such as the ACT Plan or ACT Explore contain both knowledge-based questions and interest-based questions, and use those skills and interests to determine potential careers. The Kuder Assessments, and other tests, have you rank your skills and interests to determine your ideal career path. The key point is that high school teachers and counsellors must begin to teach students that college is not the only next step after high school.

Sue did not say this but surely, she was thinking about it. We need better aptitude tests and attitude tests so that we do not overly respect a college education.

Let's bring back the Kuder tests where they have been abandoned to check aptitude in high school and stop the insistence that everybody needs to complete their life by having gone to some college someplace at some time. Let's bring back machine shop and print shop and other vocational shops for students to help them become employed right after high-school if it is right for them.

Unless you can afford the $100,000 and are willing to accept nothing in return, stay away from the College scene unless again, you are convinced that you will be in the top 25%-33%.

Sue has a head on her shoulders for sure.

Who in a debtor's prison ever has earned enough to gain their freedom? More and more student borrowers, who are already in de facto debtor's prisons see the invisible bars and choose to escape in the only way they know how. They stop paying even a dime towards their student debt and they stop answering their phone so the mean (and they are mean) credit collectors don't get them.

They see their student debt as hopeless. After a few reprieves, a few thousand 8 AM phone calls that wake-up mom and dad, several forbearances, with their debt climbing through the roof, they give up and call it quits. For a while before the end, they believe they are paying for the right to remain out of default, in much the same way they would if the dollars were borrowed from a loan shark. Then they find that they merely paid to get a forbearance and none of the debt is paid. Yes, the government loan sharks take all these payments, and none apply towards the loan. How does that help America's young adults? It makes them want to quit paying for sure.

Wen their total debt balance goes up as they send checks thinking they are paying against their debt, they finally reach a point where the alternative is a better alternative. Why bother? They default on their loans.

Eight to nine million and growing have defaulted so far and they ruined their big opportunities in life. But, paying the most they could for years without decreasing the principle was already ruining their little opportunities.

The system is unfair and once smart student borrowers know the game is rigged against them, and that they cannot get ahead, and they cannot change the system, they are smart enough to quit trying. After all they are products of the American higher education system. They know they are being ripped off.

Some want the "deadbeats" to suffer

There are those successful and somewhat lucky graduates who are not suffering from the pain of this huge debt since they have the means or the jobs to pay off their loans. I have read their comments. They do not want those less fortunate to get a break, especially if they perceive they will be paying for it or if their kids struggled with it and succeeded.

Then there are those like a person I know, whose child is now a successful doctor who got a free ride to Medical School. This person said that students, aka millennials should get no breaks on paying back student loans because his child gets nothing to defray the loan for personal expenses. Of course, interns and residents get paid about $50,000 per year to defer such expenses. And, of course doctors on the average earn about $200,000 and ER doctors earn about $300,000 per year. One more thing, graduate doctors are almost 100% assured jobs.

Though people like the person I know are in the minority, many of them are indignant that the others, not so lucky should get a small break, and surely not a big break. They have little compassion for those who do not pay their bill even if they have no job and no means of support. If they gave it little thought, they would recommend that such deadbeat borrowers should be put in debtor's prison to teach them a lesson.

They resent the fact that they had to pay off their debts on their own in order to move ahead. This is understandable to an extent but what do they want the guy or gal who they beat out for the only job in town to do?

From the Internet chatter on student loans, many that are doing well do not think that their university peers should even ask taxpayers to help them pay off their loans as it would be unfair to those, such as the fortunate with jobs, who are paying or who have paid their loans off on time.

I agree with their outrage, but the reality separates itself from their outrage. This is surely understandable, and I can appreciate having reservations about forgiving all of these debts. Yet, I believe it is best for America is we forgive them 100% and start the system over the right way. I bet I just made a few millennial friends.

It would be a good idea for those in default, those about to default, and those who ultimately will have to pay for the default to consider making the debt able to be paid without major pain. Nobody gains when the debt is rendered uncollectible and the once hopeful student's life is basically ruined for good.

None of us will ever get in line to give what is not needed to the poor, but most will help as much as we can. I like to say that I will always help the helpless, but I do not want to help make anybody helpless. Giving student loan relief is an exception.

It won't make anybody helpless. It is exactly the kind of help that can make a debt-ridden student productive for the first time in her or his life in some cases. It is good for America. From talking to the parents of students in hopeless default, I can assure you that no parent, who in good faith sent their child to higher education institutions that promised the world, expected less of a life in return. Tuition is not fair and job opportunities are gobbled up by illegal foreign nationals in many cases. Easy money through loans has a euphoric effect on the tuition overcharges that students rarely see.

Nobody expected the world in a nice basket either. However, nobody expected a life of misery after gaining their coveted degree. Meanwhile, the university and the other loan sharks including the US government long ago—all of them—have cashed the checks even though the granted degree in many cases is worthless to the graduate. Perhaps that degree is worthless to most graduates in that particular degree program. But, only the student borrower who got nothing out of it, is on the hook.

Summing it up

For hard-working students who are willing to do what they need to get into the to 25% of the class, a college loan may well be worth it. There are so many kids who cannot pay their loans back, however, that today I am inclined to think that high school seniors in the bottom 3/4 of the class, would be better off postponing full-time college and their big loans.

My best suggestion right now is to get a job for a few years and take a few courses at night until you really know that you are ready to invest $100,000 or so in loans to get you that coveted degree. God bless you in your journey.

Chapter 10 The Impact of Foreign Students

Who has skin in the student debt game?

A majority of millennials, when polled, favor unlimited immigration because *it is the right thing*. Really? For whom? Altruism is a worthwhile virtue, but self-preservation is more important. Nobody was ever documented to be able to "not survive," and be able to help legal and illegal foreign nationals take their own jobs. All altruism and all charity happen after an individual takes care of their own needs. So, I am calling out millennials to put on a good pair of life glasses and look out of their Utopia and see what they really need to survive and do well in life.

Millennials have the most skin in the student-loan game for sure. Having the right perspective on who is getting the jobs after graduation (visa overstaying foreign nationals), may prompt those with the most at stake to become rugged individualists and fight for what is theirs rather than give away all their meager possessions and become a prophet.

I must admit that I am surprised that nobody is calling out the universities for permitting more and more foreign students into their programs and then helping them gain employment ahead of unwitting American students. When foreign students graduate; guess whose jobs they take? According to their student visas, they are supposed to return to their country of origin. Once in America, however, they are not about to leave.

There are many groups that help students on their quest for employment in the US after graduating from an American university. Many foreign students come to America to stay and, so they must be employed in order to remain legally in the country. Then again, the illegal residency option is often used when students cannot find jobs in their two-month opportunity period.

International Students taking American jobs is a big problem for American students trying to get a job. Such International students are called something else after their two-month opportunity is finished. They are known as illegal foreign nationals.

Ask the university placement office for the statistics on foreign student placements and for American student placements. Do not let them include the few students who go home in the denominator. Do not let your university's administrators get away with suggesting it should not be a problem for you.

Helping foreign students is a big industry

In their senior year, the very same universities along with pillaging law firms line up to represent foreign national graduates. They make recommendations for those who want to stay in America and not go home as required by the terms of their student visas—to which they agreed and swore. International students can take any of these four options:

- ✓ Enroll in the Optional Practical Training (OPT) and work in the United States for a year
- ✓ Get an H-1B (high tech work visa) to work at an American organization
- ✓ Attend graduate school in the US while working on gaining employment

✓ Simply do not go home and work underground as an illegal resident.

✓ Whereas we most often refer to these as foreign students; the universities like to refer to them as International Students. Watch that trick designed to get American students to think less of themselves because they are not "international."!

How can a foreigner get a job in America after graduation as an International Student? There are a number of answers. Starting from the beginning, a student living in the US with an F-1 or J-1 (student) visa has 60 days to either enroll in another college or university for graduate studies or they can enroll in the OPT program to gain employment.

The *OPT* program is a very good deal for foreign students but not such a good deal for American students. It permits the J-1 and F-1 student visa status to be extended for one year so that the International student can gain professional training in their area of direct study. The application can take three to four months, so most students are advised early in their senior year to begin the process so that at graduation time, they may continue to stay in the country with employment. Their employment, by the way, may very well be the same job for which your son or daughter was aspiring. But, nobody is counting the millennial Americans who are hurt by such programs.

So, after completing all course requirements for the degree, foreign students can gain full-time employment with American companies for one year. During that year, they can work to gain an H-1B visa for the following six years. This gives up to six additional years and then they can look to extend the H-1B again or work with their company sponsor to help them gain a green card, which is non-citizen, permanent residency in the US. Meanwhile our children who demand a living wage, are waiting for the USCIS to send these job poachers home. But, they never do!

Between 2009 and 2010, as less and less Americans students were being hired, the number of *OPT* students employed in American jobs rose by 14.43 percent.

Overall, if foreign students opt to stay in the US for a longer period of time, they simply get a company to sponsor them for the H-1B non-immigrant visa. This allows them to remain employed at that company for three years, and then they can get that extended for up to six or more years.

So, as the problem for young millennial American student graduates gaining employment comes into focus, we see that a major destination for foreign students is the American workplace by achieving H-1B visas (college graduate – supposedly hi-techs).

International students from US university campuses are prime candidates for these positions. So, an innocent college education for a foreign student winds up being a job killer for American students. Yes, they do work for less. I know!

It is our Congress that permits this to occur by passing laws that are unfair to American citizens. And so, we find foreign graduates with degrees from the same universities as our children applying for jobs at the same companies that would hire our children if they were willing to work under the same conditions and for the same reduced wages as the foreign students.

Once an employer is found, the H-1B visa is granted and the foreign graduate takes the job for typically six years. Meanwhile American students go home to Mom and Dad simply to survive.

In other words, F-1, and J-1 visa holders are supposed to go home but they find university counselors or university lawyers to help get the deck stacked in their favor. They either use the OPT program or they go right to the H-1B visa program, so they do not have to go home. Because they do not go home, your millennial children cannot get jobs. Any questions?

The reason corporations hire foreigners over Americans is not because they are superior students and not that they become superior workers, but that they are a ready source of cheaper, yet still highly competent labor. Universities not only sell their foreign national graduates to corporations; they also hire more than their fair share of professors from the foreign national community. That is how I was replaced, so, I know.

Many of those hired in universities have just received graduate degrees from American universities. In other words, for financial and diversity reasons, the universities prefer not to hire Americans for the faculty jobs, which they have available. Students are taught American subjects such as American History, by foreigners who can hardly speak the American language – English! Moreover, in many cases, they have lived in America only a short while.

Congress permits colleges and universities to hire an unlimited number of foreigners as faculty or staff with the H-1B visa program. It is the exception to the nominal 65,000 H-1B visas permitted each year. American colleges and universities have a vested interest in foreign students and foreign workers. Ironically, they seem to have no such interest in Americans, who pay their salaries.

I have witnessed universities firing existing faculty to replace them with younger foreign national professors, willing to work for less money. Smaller universities will even outsource the legal part of the visa work to assure the foreign applicant receives a six-year H-1B visa. They will contract with immigration law firms and pay up to $10,000 or more per faculty member depending on the complexity of the case for the purpose of hiring a new faculty member who will work cheap for the sake of the university. How does this help American students? How does this help young millennial Americans? How does this help America? It doesn't!

Do you think that a "cheap" faculty has any effect on the quality of education our children receive? Does it have anything to do with the difficulty our children have in getting jobs?

It is really tough for Americans to get hired in US universities since our Congress has seen fit to permit an unlimited number of foreign nationals to be hired as professors or staff at universities of all sizes in the US.

With more and more debt-saturated former students not being able to survive without their parents, this also has an impact on the indebted jobless-student borrower's ability to ever consider purchasing a home.

I know that I said this already, but it is how it is, and it is worth repeating. When American college graduates begin to be hired, the housing market will begin to boom again as will the Wedding Chapel business.

This major effect on the housing market will continue for years to come until the problem with student debt is solved. Who will buy the new homes if not the young? How can a college graduate that owes the equivalent of a huge house in student loan debt, ever be considered for purchasing a home? One problem will continue to feed the other until the student debt crisis is solved. Then, homes will again be sold in America at the proper sale amount.

No solution is simple. With 30% or more former students ultimately defaulting on their loans, and many more trapped in a financial abyss, from which they may never escape, Congress can certainly create a better way to help the borrower, the housing market, and the taxpayer, all at the same time. It might not benefit foreigners or the universities, but it would help parents and the students that got sucked into promises from university pitchmen that were as powerful as the best infomercials you have ever seen on TV.

Generation Z (also known as iGeneration, Post-Millennials, or Homeland Generation) is the demographic cohort after Millennials. Whereas many millennials are the products of sloppy parenting and a few generations of *nobody at home with the kids*, Gen Z appears to be the saving solution that God has sent in the event that the Gen Y crew never get it.

When the immigration problem is solved for good in America, and it will be as Americans again choose to be Americans more than anything else, millennials who have not gotten the message will become the bus boys, the maids, and the guys and gals in the bars who refresh the stainless-steel sinks with new ice. Or they reengage in life

Currently, there are numerous additional competing names used in connection with the Z'ers in the media. There are no precise dates for when this cohort starts or ends, but demographers and researchers typically use the mid-1990s to mid-2000s as starting birth years. At the present time, there is little consensus regarding ending birth years.

Most of Generation Z have used the Internet since a young age, and they are generally comfortable with technology and with interacting on social media.

Some might suggest that all the easy solutions to the millennial problem are gone. They have been tried and they have failed. Generation Y, the millennials, have always had a major chip on their shoulders and a major sense of entitlement that they want to share with everybody. They may not produce many rock-stars in physics and nuclear technology, but they will produce more of their share of Rock Stars who have an edge against Bill Haley and the Comets. Before they attack us, let's screen them all on The Voice.

There are many examples of the utter disregard for the rest of America by disenchanted millennials, while right now, for the most part, they are sponging from America. Since millennials are tree huggers as a group. They would not approve of the many trees that would be needed if all the books on the topic of selfish, greedy, millennials were to ever be written and printed. Here are a few other opinions before we close this chapter

U.S. News & World Report is not without its opinions: *"Free Speech for Liberals Only: The Berkeley student protests against a Breitbart speaker prove there's no space for dissent against the school's liberal orthodoxy."*

Another opinion piece from Powerline: "Middlebury Prof Attacked by Mob Still Suffers From Concussion," a headline for a story giving an update on a Democratic professor assaulted by angry students for supporting a college event that featured a conservative political scientist.

That's but a few. Enough for now, though, to give rise to serious consideration of the big question:

Is there any real learning going on at America's college campuses these days? Do coffee-breath professors spend the bulk of their time preaching about the evils of America and the problems with Donald Trump? Do these bastions of academia ever have time to teach their subject matter. It sure does not seem so.

Is it possible that the four-year term that marks the typical span of post-high school higher learning has now been consumed completely by these fascists bent on training the next generation in the leftist way?

Millennials either have no brains or the mush they started with has been overtaken by coffee-breath professor infusions of the greater good. I get the feeling that millennials from Evergreen have seen and enjoyed one of my favorite T-shirts. It is a fun look with a guy and a nice cold beer as the image. It is vintage 1940's.

Evergreen, another College with grown-ups absent at the helm, condoned student rants at their white professors and the campus president. Would they no doubt feel offense at being labeled and dismissed as ignorant racists. But it is what it is. How about being civil. How about being American.

In the image on the prior page, you can see text that says simply "Beer! Give Your Brain the Night Off!" It is a great T-shirt idea but not a great life idea. Many millennials have permitted their brains to take too many nights and perhaps even too many full day's off.

So, too, all the other violence-driven student activists and radicals at America's colleges who either forget, or outright fail to recognize, what a genuine privilege it is to attend school — what a true gift and opportunity this country provides in terms of advancing one's education.

Do these negaters want to live like Third World uneducated louts? Some think maybe they already are living that way. There are plenty of spots in the world where education, particularly for girls, is on the bottom list of priorities and where it's really quite easy to skip out on even the most primary levels of schooling.

Is that what millennials want/ Why don't millennials speak up, so America hears their voices. When the millennials begin to care about America, it is possible, that America may begin to care about millennials.

Until then, maybe America needs to look for the advent of Generation Z.

These new young ones are coming right on their heels; so, millennials do not have an eternity to speak up!

So, here is a note to Evergreen anger, and to the like-minded on college campuses nationwide:

Go. Go, and leave the slots on America's college campuses for those who really want to learn — for those who don't want to waste time and lives preparing for the latest agitation, for the latest racist rant and trick of the violent activist trade.

Clearing the colleges of riffraff; bringing back the atmosphere of learning and critical thinking. That's the direction America needs to take. Absent that, college in America, for the smart crowd, at least, is nothing but a tremendous waste of time and money. God bless America!

Chapter 11: The Impact of Student Loan Debt on Millennial Happiness

Forbes.com By Sarah Landrum Oct 20, 2017, 02:59pm

I have included the entirety of Sarah Lundrum's article in Forbes knowing that Forbes and Sarah would like to help all millennials. After all, Millennials are people too!

Please enjoy this piece as I have. It is right to the point. Though there are many other issues that Millennials face, besides student debt, the massive amount of debt they carry is a very negative force in their lives. Relieving millennials of this burden can solve many problems. Here goes:

Student loan debt is costing millennials more than their financial freedom.

There are many kinds of freedom, but very freedoms are possible to achieve without financial dignity.

Maybe it's not surprising that scientists have spent time studying the impact of various kinds of debt on the human psyche. Buying, selling and managing debt is, after all, a multi-billion-dollar-a-year industry. It's a huge cornerstone of the world economy. Don't we deserve to fully understand the influence it wields over our lives?

The rate at which college students are graduating with debt today is literally approaching crisis levels. Unsurprisingly, not all of the long-term costs are about money.

Students debt and the real costs of college

Recent psychological research into how earnings and debt influence our waking minds reveals that the size of our paychecks is, practically speaking, immaterial if we're not already on sound financial footing. In other words: Debt is a happiness killer. None of us can be truly happy if we're saddled with debt.

Additional research and polling reveal that the specter of student loan debt nearly extinguishes the joy we associate with graduating from college in the first place. When Gallup administered this poll and published the subsequent findings, they discovered something else: a kind of "tipping point" where the accrual of personal debt shifts from "acceptable investment" to "source of existential dread." According to the pollsters, that point is around the $25,000-mark.

At the present time, the average American household with student debt owes about $49,000. Graduates in their twenties spend more than $350 per month, on average, on student loan payments and interest. Since the average "entry-level" job was worth about $50,000 a year in 2016 for new graduates, "truly average" college grads in America can expect to see their earnings garnished by between eight and 10% for roughly ten to twelve years after they graduate.

That's a lot of averages and assumptions, but it's still instructive. It tells us that the problem is not necessarily about debt itself, but rather the proportion of our earnings it represents, the size it takes on in our imaginations and, therefore, the toll it takes on our mental health.

All valuable things in life are worth paying for in some fashion, but the place student loan occupies in society at the present moment is beginning to feel like a cascade failure.

It all begins with a pretty simple but ultimately false assumption: College is valuable and must, therefore, cost a lot of money.

We're not at a place right now where we can start talking about "free" colleges — even if "free" actually means "included in the cost of paying taxes" — on the national level. Some states, like New York, are showing how such a thing can be done, but we're not remotely there at the federal level.

Additionally, there will always be a place in the world for "deluxe" colleges because there will always be folks who are willing to pay "deluxe" prices to be there. But for everybody else, it just makes good moral and economic sense to lower the barrier of entry until attending college is an attainable dream for all of us.

There are lots of reasons why the idea of a "debt industry" leaves a sour taste in our mouths, not all of which require vigorous scientific scrutiny. So here's a non-scientific way to look at student debt and how it applies to a happy and harmonious society.

America has always been billed as a meritocracy. This is a place where everybody who wishes to participate can spend some effort improving themselves — by pursuing education or employment, say — and then receive a commensurate "reward" in exchange for that effort. If you spend time and energy building a small business or learning skills in college to prepare yourself for the next-higher run on the ladder, for example, society ought to have mechanisms in place which reward you for that effort.

But there's the problem: When we're talking about college — the accrual of knowledge — effort should be the bulk of the "buy-in" required rather than money. The shared dream of lifting ourselves by our bootstraps should be attainable for all who possess the wish to improve themselves even if they do not necessarily have the means.

In practical terms, this means investing as a society in grants and subsidies for prospective students who come from poor and middle-income households through no fault of their own. Unfortunately, even this simple proposal — the idea that we invest in future generations with our tax dollars — is anathema in our current political climate. There are federally subsidized loans, grants, scholarships and other forms of assistance available to those who know where to look, but actors in America's ultraconservative government are chipping away at these programs in the name of budget reconciliation.

Meritocracy was never supposed to be an exclusive country club. Ideally, no student should be expected to work more than a few hours a week while pursuing a full-time education. The costs of attending college have risen ceaselessly for an entire generation, and doubling-down now on the myth that it's only for the well-to-do or liberals or elitists is not going to help solve that problem. Human knowledge must be shared, or else it becomes worthless. Attaining a future where anyone can pursue higher learning without ruining their financial standing or their sanity should be high on our list of shared priorities now and always.

End of article

Sarah Landrum is right. It would be great for tuition to be very affordable. But that is not the direction in which colleges and universities are heading. Community Colleges and small inexpensive colleges would work but that is not what we have today. It would take a major national commitment and a change in attitude to get students and parents to give up their favorite private schools even if the cost were free. But, if the cost were free, we could eliminate the notion of student loan debt completely.

Even small private schools today such as my great Alma Mater King's College and other private schools such as Misericordia University, Marywood University, Scranton University, Baptist Bible College, and Wilkes University are not building buildings at a torrid pace, so they can reduce costs. King's for example was $450 per semester in 1965 when I attended and today it is $17,500 per semester without fees. It is one of the least expensive private institutions in Northeastern PA.

Of course, students in the bottom of the class and those who do not want to specialize in what colleges teach would do well to skip college for several years until 21-yaars of age of older and then perhaps by then, they will already have a great career rather than a pile of debt.

Having no debt as Sarah says is one way to avoid a major "source of existential dread."
d

Chapter 12 The Big Millennial Summary

Millennials filled up this book

As we discussed in this book, millennials have enough issues to fill up a book, which we already have done. The book of course needed to begin at their birth when a former hippy mommy and daddy brought these little angels into a world in which Kindergarten values no longer mattered. Additionally, the heartwarming stories on the Hallmark Channel were deemed to be bogus, and the only recognized path to success was being able to snag participation trophies for breathing right, with a major caution to not have too many or Johnny next door might get upset.

Yes, as junior and juniorette grew up, after few lessons at home, they were gifted with one participation trophy after another. Awarding millennial children trophies for merely participating in sports or any type of events was the first of many misguided cultural practices that would ultimately lead to the demise of this entire generation. At home they were told they were the best even though they were not.

While at school, they were told they could do anything they wanted; they were told they were smart and capable and entitled to the whole world. In a result that surprised everyone but shouldn't have, a generation raised to get high on its own esteem grew into a bunch of lost adults. Today's young Americans, who preceded the Z-generation for whom there is great hope, have been disappointed by reality and they are still incapable of taking the smallest amount of responsibility for their role in it.

The old Atari and Vic20 and the Commodore 64 home computers helped the very young millennials on their way up with math and other skills while the TI-99-4A helped them learn how to Hunt the Wumpus. The next set of technology, however, did them in. The rise of the Internet and powerful cell-phones hurt them in their ability to become complete adults. The older generations noticed that full conversations had been reduced to text messages, and personalities to avatars.

Personal interaction is almost all gone. It was sacrificed over and over because it was more convenient to do it alone with the technology than in person. All character-building friction has been chopped away from the everyday millennial experience, and the results are pathetic.

Not everything in real life is rosy. The millennials have had their shoes tied by somebody else for too many years for them to have become rugged individuals. Some might say that these lounge-lizard-like blobs of semi-lifelessness have replaced what could have been able-bodied adults.

This group of *less-than is OK people* has little time for arcane notions such as values and morals and attributes like kindness and self-discipline, and of course hard work. Hard work is one of the biggest failings of these young Americans.

The online paradigm shift replaced these old notions with superficial measures such as beauty, money, fame and followers. Millennials have even figured out how to measure these things. As a result, narcissism has become the order of the day. Me, Myself, & I!

Managers in the workplace when asked about them use a number of negative words to describe them. The adjectives they overwhelmingly shouted out — as if recited — were "privileged, narcissistic, entitled, spoiled, job hopping "Trophy Kids" backed up with "irresponsible, and of course unreliable.

This group of what some might call future-slugs and snails go off to college and sometimes they enter the working and grown up worlds. Never having to fight for their own space as children, they enter like squealing puppies, experiencing their first night alone in the spare room.

Ironically their self-esteem is typically high from their trophy room and with fantasies validated by electronic "likes." After years of the façade, more than a few smarten up and they conclude after a while that they'd like a life other than their own. But, in their world, they would be crushed if they had to admit it.

The most concerning part of it all, though, is that so many of us have failed to identify the real crux of the millennial problem. For Boomers, let me tell you what it is. It is us. Yes, we did it to them.

The millennials are notably materialistic. Though they typically cannot fund even their own materialism, they have developed a reputation for a certain desire for material things.

Their relationship with money is quite simple. They do not have much of it, and what they do have; they are reluctant to spend. That makes sense. They are non-participants in commerce, partly because of their student loan debt and partly because it is how they think.

They buy fewer cars and houses, and even though they love electronics to support their cultural needs, they cannot spend beyond their limited means. Their credit-card debt has declined, more than likely because they cannot get a credit card, and for some because they had at one time filed bankruptcy.

Ironically, millennials, when polled, remain optimistic about their futures. Those non-millennials, who analyze their plight have a fear that this group of lost Americans may actually have entered a situation in which permanently lower earnings and lower savings is a part of their future. They are destined to spend less and save less. They may be the best-educated generation ever, but they need some help in parenting so that their children have a chance at life.

As discussed plenty in this book, millennial politics is simple. Young Americans just a bit older than the Generation-Z conservative contingent growing up behind them, support big government, unless they get a job and have to pay taxes. They are also for smaller government, unless some lack of funding affects them. They trust Washington and Democratic Politicians implicitly. They count on Washington to fix everything, as long as it doesn't try to run anything like a business.

When Washington fails them, they listen intently to the political spin from the press and they never blame the politicians that have worsened their plight. They are a strange lot indeed—one paradox after another. And, by the way don't waste your time asking them for help.

They say that a metamorphosis happens to their thinking when by happenchance, they become employed or win the Lottery and either begin to make a lot of money or have a ton given to them. Millennials begin to get quite squeamish about giving any away— even to their friends in big government.

OK nobody's perfect; we must help them!

We hold up a broad brush when we paint the color "millennial" as a nasty color for sure. To Baby Boomers, they are simply distasteful in many ways. Yet, they are from us and we failed them. We the Boomers failed the millennials. Yes, that is right. We did. Then we painted them a nasty color.

They did not crawl out of the womb any different than we did. But, our moms and dads treated us better. Boomers and need some make up time for our millennial offspring. They are ours. Not all are the same but, good and bad, they are ours. We could have done better.

Sure, there are many stuck in their terrible 22's. From 22 to 30-somethings, some actually are doing fine. They are already operating as entrepreneurs and innovators—using the trademarked energy and curiosity of youth to shape the world. There are many more forging the foundations of successful adult careers, but the millennial malcontents get all the publicity.

For having done little to assure their success and by abandoning them now when they are not the apples of everyone's eyes, we, their elders, are at fault. We, who are prone to immediately disqualify any achievers from millennial status, had better wise up and figure out how to make it right by them. We cannot keep reserving the term millennial exclusively for the terrible 22's and older, who are the malcontents.

Let's give it a try Boomers. Let's not keep guaranteeing the generational identity of this group of young Americans to remain negative. To say it again as I have often repeated in this book, the painful truth is that we, their elders did not do enough and what we have done since, has fashioned the keepers of that now negative identity.

It was us. We raised them; and we failed them, and we keep failing them. Now, many of us are so busy keeping them locked up behind a hopelessly negative boilerplate, that we have become the oppressors of an entire generation. It was us. We led them toward the sort of character that we got from them when we could have led them towards something that none of us could so easily disrespect.

Do they deserve a break? We're talking about a whole generation of young people. They are our children. Of course, they deserve a break. They deserve their redemption. We owe it to them. We must provide it.

Let's start the ball rolling by insisting the government redirect some of its new-found oil and gas revenues and forgive all of the student loans that are on the books. All of them—and then never let anybody 17 or 18 years of age ever get in over their heads like that again. That was our fault, too. Then, they can all begin their lives—not just the top ¼ of the class.

Then let's do what we know how to do well. Let's review our own Kindergarten lessons and watch a few more good Hallmark shows and figure out what we can do other than cast aspersions. Let's help turn around something that we caused. Instead of facing something nobody would wish on anybody, let's permit and encourage millennials to face a bright future in a loving America.

I say, "Let's not give up on young Americans. We can instead, make their lives much better." What do you say? Let's do it together.

Other books by Brian Kelly: (<small>amazon.com, and Kindle</small>)

Great Coaches in Pittsburgh Steelers Football Sixteen of the best coaches ever to coach in pro football.
Great Moments in New England Patriots Football Great football moments from Boston to New England
Great Moments in Philadelphia Eagles Football. The best from the Eagles from the beginning of football.
Great Moments in Syracuse Football The great moments, coaches & players in Syracuse Football
Boost Social Security Now! Hey Buddy Can You Spare a Dime?
The Birth of American Football. From the first college game in 1869 to the last Super Bowl
Obamacare: A One-Line Repeal Congress must get this done.
A Wilkes-Barre Christmas Story A wonderful town makes Christmas all the better
A Boy, A Bike, A Train, and a Christmas Miracle A Christmas story that will melt your heart
Pay-to-Go America-First Immigration Fix
Legalizing Illegal Aliens Via Resident Visas Americans-first plan saves $Trillions. Learn how!
60 Million Illegal Aliens in America!!! A simple, America-first solution.
The Bill of Rights By Founder James Madison Refresh *your knowledge of the specific rights for all*
Great Players in Army Football Great Army Football played by great players..
Great Coaches in Army Football Army's coaches are all great.
Great Moments in Army Football Army Football at its best.
Great Moments in Florida Gators Football Gators Football from the start. This is the book.
Great Moments in Clemson Football CU Football at its best. This is the book.
Great Moments in Florida Gators Football Gators Football from the start. This is the book.
The Constitution Companion. A Guide to Reading and Comprehending the Constitution
The Constitution by Hamilton, Jefferson, & Madison – Big type and in English
PATERNO: The Dark Days After Win # 409. Sky began to fall within days of win # 409.
JoePa 409 Victories: Say No More! Winningest Division I-A football coach ever
American College Football: The Beginning From before day one football was played.
Great Coaches in Alabama Football Challenging the coaches of every other program!
Great Coaches in Penn State Football the Best Coaches in PSU's football program
Great Players in Penn State Football The best players in PSU's football program
Great Players in Notre Dame Football The best players in ND's football program
Great Coaches in Notre Dame Football The best coaches in any football program
Great Players in Alabama Football from Quarterbacks to offensive Linemen Greats!
Great Moments in Alabama Football AU Football from the start. This is the book.
Great Moments in Penn State Football PSU Football, start--games, coaches, players,
Great Moments in Notre Dame Football ND Football, start, games, coaches, players
Cross Country with the Parents A great trip from East Coast to West with the kids
Seniors, Social Security & the Minimum Wage. Things seniors need to know.
How to Write Your First Book and Publish It with CreateSpace
The US Immigration Fix--It's all in here. Finally, an answer.
I had a Dream IBM Could be #1 Again The title is self-explanatory
WineDiets.Com Presents The Wine Diet Learn how to lose weight while having fun.
Wilkes-Barre, PA; Return to Glory Wilkes-Barre City's return to glory
Geoffrey Parsons' Epoch... The Land of Fair Play Better than the original.
The Bill of Rights 4 Dummmies! This is the best book to learn about your rights.
Sol Bloom's Epoch ...Story of the Constitution The best book to learn the Constitution
America 4 Dummmies! All Americans should read to learn about this great country.
The Electoral College 4 Dummmies! How does it really work?
The All-Everything Machine Story about IBM's finest computer server.
ThankYou IBM! This book explains how IBM was beaten in the computer marketplace by neophytes

Brian has written 163 books in total. Other books can be found at amazon.com/author/brianwkelly

www.ingramcontent.com/pod-product-compliance
Lightning Source LLC
Chambersburg PA
CBHW060907280326
41934CB00007B/1216